for my Rosemary
with love,
   Roßy 5-14-06
   Olson

D0923308

REFLECTIONS OF THE HEART

THE INTERNATIONAL LIBRARY OF PHOTOGRAPHY

PICTURE.COM

L. Clerkin, Editor

Reflections of the Heart

Copyright © 2005
by The International Library of Photography
as a compilation.

Rights to individual photographs reside with the photographers themselves.
This collection of photographs contains works submitted to the Publisher by individual photographers who confirm that the work is their original creation. Based upon the photographer's confirmation and to the Publisher's actual knowledge, these photographs were taken by
the listed photographers. The International Library of Photography does not guarantee or
assume responsibility for verifying authorship of each work.

The views expressed within certain photographs contained in this anthology do not necessar-
ily reflect the views of the editors or staff of The International Library of Photography.

All rights reserved under International and Pan-American copyright conventions. No part of
this book may be reproduced, stored in a retrieval system or transmitted in any form, electronic, mechanical, or by other means, without written permission of the publisher. Address
all inquiries to Jeffrey Bryan, 3600 Crondall Lane, Suite 101, Owings Mills, MD 21117.

Library of Congress
Cataloging in Publication Data

ISBN 0-7951-5261-2

Printed in China

Published by
The International Library of Photography
3600 Crondall Lane
Suite 101
Owings Mills, MD 21117

FOREWORD

Writing about photography is a difficult task, as it entails the translation of one art form into another. While every photograph may not inspire a thousand words, it is easy to see how the saying evolved. Words are a function of the intellect. But, much like music, a visual image speaks directly to the emotions, evoking an immediate and powerful response. Only when one attempts to analyze, interpret, and critique this image do words come into play.

As one views a photograph, one is slowly taken on a visual journey through the eye of the photographer. Whether the photograph was staged or the "point-and-click method" was employed, the picture represents the fact that moments in time pass within the blink of an eye. The photographer not only captures a scene or a subject; he also creates a lasting, tangible image of a fleeting instant. The beauty of photography is that any individual can produce an image of these passing moments.

Photography represents both an active and a passive art form. The degree to which a photographer participates in his art form varies from photograph to photograph. The photographer can either tell a story within the photograph, or simply stand aside and record life as it happens. The one thing that holds true for all photography is this: without the photographer there can be no photograph. Even in a simple snapshot, the photographer's influence is clearly evident.

The photographs within this anthology exhibit their own importance as well as demonstrate the importance of the photographer. In some cases, the idea or photo found the photographer. For instance, while taking pictures on a nature hike, a photographer may catch the sunset as it breaks through a bunch of trees, and thus an idea may be born. In other instances, a photographer may orchestrate and choreograph the set-up of a photograph in order to fulfill a creative idea or notion. (This may be the case in still-life or abstract photography.)

Another similar element in most of these photographs is the photographer's love of and dedication to his subject. For example, nature photography is often captured by devoted nature watchers. Those people who take humorous photographs usually enjoy the lighter side of life and tend to look for the funniest aspect of any situation. The numerous photographs of children in this book were most likely taken by parents or grandparents who appreciate the joy and wonderment contained in a child's smile. Becoming emotionally involved with a subject, through deep love or interest, often enables a photographer to generate ideas that help him capture the true essence of his subject.

There are also photographers who gain inspiration not from relating to one specific subject or another, but rather from focusing on the photographic process itself. They often use special techniques to create images they have envisioned within their own minds, or they choose to concentrate on one particular aspect of photography (such as lighting) and through experimentation examine its effect on a particular subject. By casting aside conventional approaches, these photographers open different pathways to new ideas, allowing their own imaginations to roam freely.

No matter how or why a photograph is taken, the viewer must realize that each photograph represents an individual's artistic viewpoint. There are many excellent photographs contained in this anthology. At a quick glance they might appear to be just pictures, but be sure to focus on the ideas being conveyed, both emotionally and physically. Allow yourself to become lost in the photo: perhaps you may gain a new understanding of it, or you may simply be able to relate more deeply to the photographer's viewpoint.

Andy Warhol once predicted that in the future everyone will have his fifteen minutes in the spotlight. This philosophy could easily be applied to photography by simply stating that every subject has its moment, and as a photographer, one must strive to find and capture these instants. After all, these cherished moments, which may seem frozen in time when we see them through the camera's viewfinder, do not last fifteen minutes; rather, viewing a photograph that captures these instances may trigger memories that will always remain embedded deep within our minds. Through photographs we are therefore offered a physical reminder as an accompaniment to a memory. We then hold in our hands the permanency of a cherished moment in time—an image of yesterday.

Russell Hall
Senior Editor

Paula A. Eakins   Nature
Taking It All In

Sharon Riddle   Animals/Pets
Alex

Joy Adams   People
Untitled

Beverly Odell   People
Sneaking

Megan Dudley   People
Sweet Dreams

Marci Willenbrink   Humor
Little Cowboy

Mildred Turoff　　　　　　　　　Animals/Pets
Flower, Cat, Kittens

Shelby E. Van Arkel　　　　　　　Nature
Serenity

Charles Binkowitz　　　　　　　People
Community Relation

Elaine Matsuda　　　　　　　　Nature
Pink Surprise

Avi M. Wizenfelf　　　　　　　Nature
Lonely

Rena Adams　　　　　　　　Animals/Pets
Togetherness

Barbara A. Bishop People
Hugs And Kisses

Gloria Gibbs People
Is This Where I Dress It?

Anthony Fama Nature
Tranquility

Nancy Queen Action
The Maid Of The Mist

Clifford A. DePass Nature
God's Crescendo

Freda I. Bullett Humor
First Things First

Dennell Guyette People
Untitled

David R. Jones Nature
Autumn In Edinburgh

James Weber Nature
Cheeze

Jane Taffe Nature
Nature's Colorful Carpet

Megan Wright Animals/Pets
The Grinning Crocodile

Douglas E. Wollaston Nature
Sunrise In Morgan Hill

Frankie Mahannah Children
Girl Play With Tiger!

Alicia Leighton Nature
Bridge Over Quiet Waters

Steve Heath Animals/Pets
Man's Best Friend?

Lorraine Szapka Children
Brothers And Baseball

James T. Duff Nature
A Unique Tree

Carol Brownell Sports
The Comfort Of Fishing

Austin Michael   People
Sliding Into Fall

Michelle D. Fimbel   Other
Window To History, University Of Tampa

April Randall   Nature
August Sunrise

Sharon Baggett   Travel
Summer's Be

Nancy Bryce   Animals/Pets
Ride The Waves

Lee Carley   People
Mother And Daughter

Jennifer Fierro Nature
White Calm

Karen S. Brewer Other
The Waiting Thaw

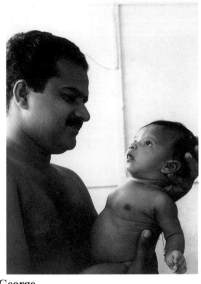

Thomas A. George People
First Heart-To-Heart Talk With Dad

Victor Hugo Herrera People
Men At Work

Jill Kelly Children
First Time At The Beach

Traci Smith Children
Morning Son

Annette Kiker　　　　　　　　　　Children
Gracie Cooling Off

Kathy Peach　　　　　　　　　　Other
The Longest Icicle

Marilyn Eckles　　　　　　　　　　Children
That's My Boy

Kimberly Wilson　　　　　　　　　　Children
Christmas In Hawaii

William L. Feldmann　　　　　　　　　　Children
A Brother's Love

Rose Iezzi　　　　　　　　　　Children
Fishing For Daddy

Lisa McLaughlin   Nature
Naples Pier Sunset

Rob Carney   Humor
Take A Chance

Beth Bush   Children
Hi Andrea!

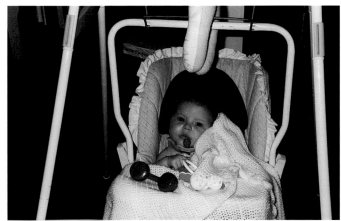

Cheryl Koboldt   Children
Ahh, Home At Last!

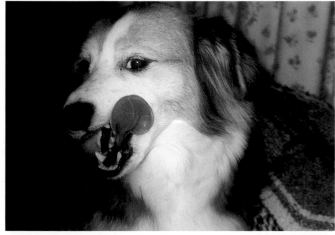

Russ & Teresa Lopes   Animals/Pets
Missed A Spot

Helena Rozbicka   People
Mother And Child

Rose Scott   Children
Night Sleepers

Iris Bertoglio   Animals/Pets
Sunning Herself

Alois J. Petrzel   Animals/Pets
NBC

Aimee L. Haynes   Nature
Sunrise On The Gulf

Gigi Republica   Children
Me And Scraffy

Susan McCartney   Children
Reflections

Donald D. Frantz   Travel
Base Of American Falls

Cindy Black   Children
First Easter

Terri L. Watkins   Animals/Pets
The Catnip Is Greener On The Other Side

Marlene T. Wiercioch   Children
Howling Friends

Helen Thomsen   Nature
Fall In Court House Park

James Julian   Nature
Snow On Copley

Marydith Newman Travel
Elephants Of Amboseli

Barbara Hornyak Animals/Pets
Are You Sure You Can't See Me?

Alexandra M. McKenzie Children
Bonnie Wee Lass

Stella M. Steffy Animals/Pets
And Is Greatly Missed!

Frances R. Johnson Animals/Pets
The Future Belongs To The Children

Patricia Gregory Children
Shade On A Sunny Day

Dennis G. Cook   Action
RJ Diving In Our Pool

Lisa Ferraro   Animals/Pets
Meaghan At Paradise Lake

Noreen Colannino   Other
Sweet Emotion

Vivian Barden   Nature
Potomac Sunrise

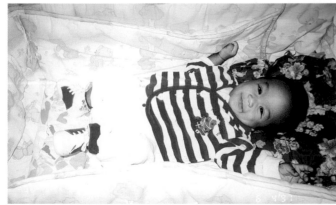

Hai Vo   Children
The Smile For Daddy Action

Donna Fazzino   Nature
Grand Canyon, Arizona

Vanessa Quate People
Man Of God

Kim Koenemann Animals/Pets
Brutus

Anna Sullivan Children
Story Time

Stephanie M. Mina Animals/Pets
Untitled

Nancy Lyon Wright Nature
My Time Of Day

Margaret Hagerman Travel
Reflections: Vietnam Veterans Memorial

Hailee Murray   Children
Another Day At The Beach

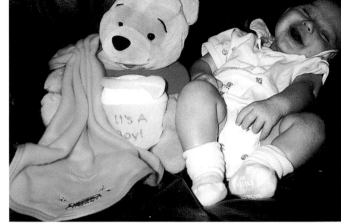

Bretta Kelly   Children
Pooh Smiling

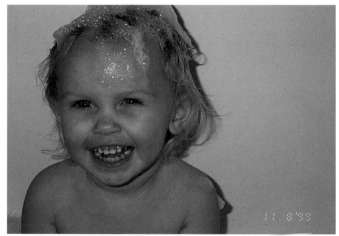

Gabrielle Lutterbuck   Children
It's Bubble Time

Bethany Bares   Children
Let It Snow

Tammy Oster   Children
Fall Foliage

Doyle Nichols   Animals/Pets
Almost Chow Time

Jennifer Smith Nature
Ghosts Of The River

Linda M. Haeseker Children
Halloween Fun

Edna C. Castro Nature
Untitled

Alois J. Petrzel Travel
Beach Day, Cape Cod

Debbi Kaplan Nature
Beauty Beyond The Trees

Frankie Enochs Animals/Pets
Afternoon Nap

Jenita B. Norotsky   Travel
Shine

Shirley V. Schuetz   Nature
Lighting The Way

Susan K. Lottig   Children
Texas, Sad Bluebonnets

Bev Nuss   Children
Yeah, Got 'Er Done

Paula Mutzberg   Other
Train To Nowhere

Donna Lubus   Children
Serene, Peaceful

Teresa Conner   Animals/Pets
Friendly Snooze

Lauren Leneice Frasier   Nature
Reflections

Barbara Frost   Travel
Sphinx, Pyramid

Lynette Rimmer   Children
Clean Feet

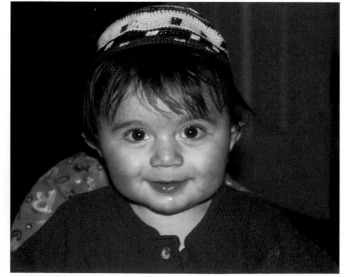

Tamara Cornieux   Children
Sweet Pea

Anna Roseman   Nature
Heavenly Awakening

Steve Diehn Children
Jessica, Autumn Beauty

Cynthia Caruso Animals/Pets
Frankie

Joyce Felske Nature
God's Handiwork

Susan Whatley Children
Best Friends

Aileen Mobley Children
Happy Reflection

Nicholas E. Moccia Children
Jester Little Angel

Kathy Grugnale   Children
Stranded At The Altar

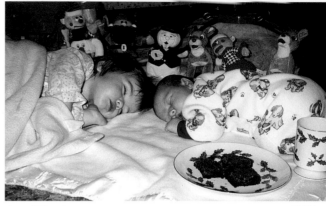

Amy Marrier   Children
Waiting For Santa

Raven Rodriguez   Children
Let It Snow

Sonya Kaiser   Children
Summer Fun

Michele Kober-Holcomb   Children
It's Not My Feet That Smell

Deanna Eldredge   Children
Apple Picking

Don Pidich   Nature
Llama

Ellen Hempel   Children
Big Brother Meets Little Sis

Ryan Patton   Other
Window To The Past

Karen McAlister   Nature
Arrowhead Anticipation

Brian Lammey   Action
Hang Time

Amy Henderson   Children
My Little Cowgirl

Dawn Cantleberry   Animals/Pets
Hammock Full Of Fur

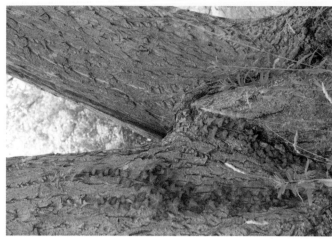

Lucelly Londoño   Nature
Humanized Nature

Joe & Debbie Vega   Animals/Pets
When Do I Eat My Cake?

Irene M. Byczek   Nature
Sky In Awe

Mary Jane Perrotti   Children
A Bubble Bath In The Bucket

Clarissa Gosciej   Nature
Spring Mountains

Vicki Anderson   Nature
St. Helen's

Michele Howerton   Children
Mama's Adorable Gift

Lisa McWhirter   Children
Sophisticated Devil: Michael McWhirter

Laura Kahler   Travel
Colorful Jamaica

Robin Sibert   Children
Mykie Rose

Geneva A. Bugg   Children
A Boy And His Dog

Deborah MacDougal Animals/Pets
Christmas Eve

Kathleen Oriti Travel
Pittsburgh Sunset

Connie S. Runyon Nature
Nature's Twist

Michael Walter Sunday Travel
Heidelberg Castle View

Barbara Schapel People
Young And Old, Ireland

Eugene Keener Children
My Girls!

Michelle Renton   Children
Keeping Cool

Nydirah Cheeks   Children
Three Little Fingers

Amanda M. Turner   Children
Worn Out

Evelyn Maxwell   Nature
Sunflowers

Kimberly Breen   Children
Untitled

Veronica Livescu   Nature
After Rain

Marysol Guerrero   Travel
Exploring The Mayas

Tonya A. Hartsell   Travel
USS Battleship, North Carolina

Jay Scott Hernandez   Travel
Sunrise Serenity In Palm Beach, Florida

Charles Dashiell   Nature
Honduran Sunset

Candace Fisher   Nature
Sunset

Athena Athanasiou   Children
All About Me

Raechele Damschen   Children
Brother Love

Juanita Jackson   Animals/Pets
Gotcha, Mr. Frog

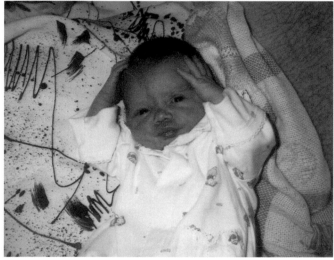

Christine Baird   Children
Oh No, Not Another Picture Again!

Don D. Jensen   Nature
High Country Oasis

Donya Kato   People
The Judge

Ryan Notch   Nature
Three Palms

Nicholas P. Lanteri   People
Graduation

Tracey Elder   Children
Bundle Of Joy

Vernessa LuShaun Burgess   Animals/Pets
A Whale Of A Time At Miami Seaquarium

Kierra Robinson   Children
Going Trick-Or-Treating

Paolo Polidori   Nature
Nuova Vita: New Life

Dana Payne   Children
Angel From Heaven

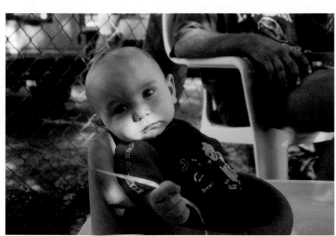

Sheri Brennan   Children
First Birthday

Tracey Seenath   Children
Breanna: Future Wedding Pose

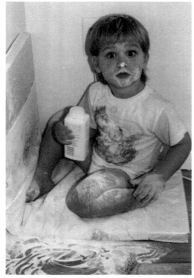

Debbie A. Lancaster   Children
It Wasn't Me!

Caroline Grinage   Nature
Fall's Brilliance

Deborah Culbertson   Children
Hey Buddy

Leslie Hall   Children
A Day In The Garden

Pam Nehls   Nature
Statue In The Garden: Charleston, SC

Marco Po   Nature
Luci

Dendra Lee Ferrari   Children
Dominic's Surprise

Tessa K. Ferrario   Other
Floor Watch

Beverly Sue Tate   Nature
New Year's Day In Southern California

Terry Legge   Children
So Cool

Kim Simpson   Portraiture
Little Lady

Ranie Rieta   Children
Roll Over, Fiona

David Ducharme   Nature
Water Slide

Annie M. Hayhurst   Children
Dandy

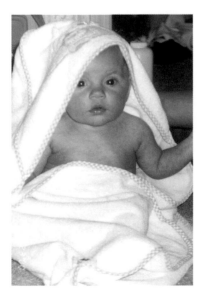

Jeff Yates   Children
Untitled

Sumeet Shashikant Shevade   Nature
Nature's Beauty

Ford Kim Portraiture
Bridge Off The Port

Jeannette S. LeBar Children
Cool Dude

Joao Filipe Barbosa Nature
Sunset By The Lake

Dave John Stubberfield Travel
Leeds Castle From Above

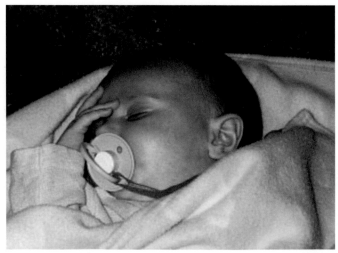

Denise Marie Marcier Children
Life Is So Hard

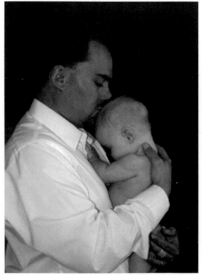

Charlotte Ann Brodie Portraiture
My Girl

Donald R. Dodge Children
Halloween Charmer

Nathalie Nikolovski Children
Is Summer Always This Hot?

Laurie Drum Children
Nap Time

Andrea Nemes Children
Andrea Going For A Joyride In The Summer

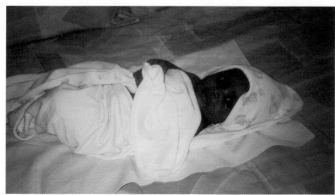

Kamaree Malik Manuel Children
A Special Moment

Teri Davis Children
Our New Angel

Amy Lane Children
Just A Floating

Deborah J. Scoggin Animals/Pets
Jimmy

Paul Dobias Animals/Pets
Malamute Finds Ice On A Hot Summer Day

Debra Stacy Comella Nature
Garden Of The Groves

Colleen Radcliffe Children
Sisterly Secrets

Ben Wayne Olson Animals/Pets
Life And Death On The Kitchen Floor

Lynn Fleming — Animals/Pets
Untitled

Kimberly R. Sirek — Animals/Pets
Hildagard Florentina

Kim Foder — Nature
Summer Afternoon

Brenda L. Bihlear — People
My Girl

Jennifer L. Schmitt Price — Travel
Kenora, Ontario

Cookie Morales — Animals/Pets
Togetherness

Denise Diane Andersen   Animals/Pets
This Month's Cover Of FQ (Feline Quarterly)

Pamela Ware   Other
Sunset On 660

Patricia Ann Coffaro   Nature
Untitled

Elicia E. Kelley   Nature
A Child's Love

Nancy Gregory   Nature
Mountains

Kayla Garaway   People
BFF Twins

Debra B. Bisson　　　　　　　　Children
Brandon Rests

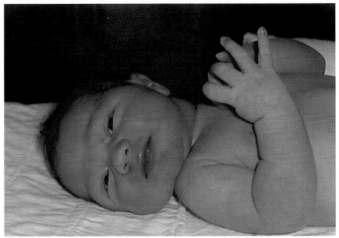

Glenda Bishop　　　　　　　　Children
Welcome To The World

Susan Brimmer　　　　　　　　Children
Falling Leaves

Christi G. Opstrup　　　　　　Children
Just Hanging Out

Kathryn Bigelow　　　　　　　Children
The Pumpkin Patch

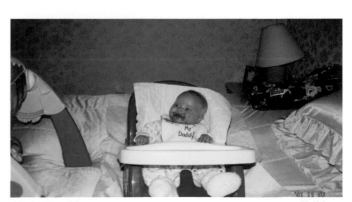

Silvia Hutchinson　　　　　　Children
I Love Carrots

Tammy Ellenburg   Children
Untitled

Chris Francis   Children
Splash

Tami Dolezal Cotton   Children
Our Little Pumpkin

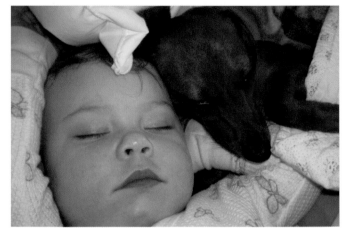

Janet B. Hill   Children
Sweet Dreams

Diane Medina   Children
Stuck On You

Ester Adele Jones   Children
Baby Bunny

Laura Sutherland   Children
Princess Jordan Is Hoping This Frog Will Be A Prince!

Debra Beatrice Bisson   Travel
Spring In British Columbia

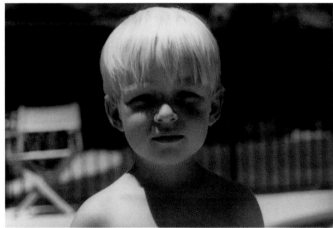

Kathryn Ellen Bogner   Children
Innocence

Doug Sudduth   Nature
Ledger Sighting #3

V. A. Kirchofer   Children
Mama's Pride And Joy

Dani Elizabeth Davis   People
Shine On Me

Diana Mary Schenkel   People
Jennifer

James Hutchinson   Nature
Painted With Light

James Degregorio   Nature
Yosemite's Greatness

Sylvia Garofalo   Action
Lift Off!

Sean Evans   Children
Eyes Of The Innocent

Robin Renee Weaver   Nature
Garden Gate

Douglas Ray Clifford   Nature
Full Moon

Carla Gois   Children
Angel

Adrienn Ida Menes   Nature
Red Dream

William J. Edmondson   Children
Puppy Love

Sherrie Ann Lambaren   Animals/Pets
All Dressed Up

Katrina F. Huddy   Children
Friendship

Jennifer Lynn Christopher   Children
One Nation Under God

Spring LaShell Wolf   Children
Strike A Pose

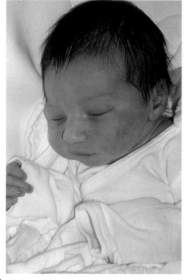

Elisa Marie Ranze   Children
Dillan Ranze: 7/13/02 (Day Of Birth)

Jason Allen Blowe   Travel
Blue Ridge

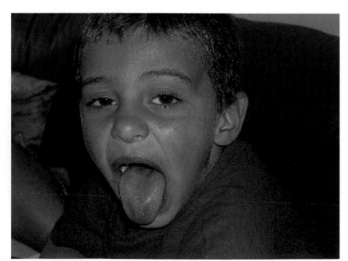

Genevieve M. Piturro   Children
Christopher's Green Lollipop

Laura Jo Wolfe   Animals/Pets
As Good As It Gets

Tami Lynn Brown   Animals/Pets
When's Santa Coming?

Delores Jean Foulks   Animals/Pets
Cherub

Leslie S. Flynton   Animals/Pets
Riley In The Bag

Shirley Ann Hershberger   Animals/Pets
Curious Puppies

Jamie Mishelle Ashcraft   Animals/Pets
Tiffany, That Cutie

David G. Snow   Other
The Face Of Destitution

Diane Barbara Levy　　　　　　　　　　Nature
Beautiful Flowers At The Historic Gardens

Sean M. Guilfoyle　　　　　　　　　　Travel
Sunset Over Kauai

Michele Barrall　　　　　　　　　　Children
Innocence

Gene Wang　　　　　　　　　　People
Surprise!

Gina Diane Bouchard　　　　　　　　　　Nature
Lake Tahoe

Mal E. Durbin　　　　　　　　　　Other
Relaxing In Brecon

Jean Souza Lopes — Other
Light And Shadow

Sharon Susan Mclean — Portraiture
Shaz Glamour

Brennan J. Hill — Nature
Muir Woods

LaDawn Cecelia Bryce — Nature
Oregon Sunset

Chris Allan Wynn — Nature
Dock

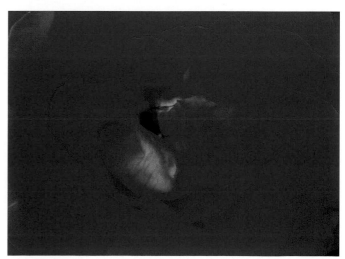

Alex Golimbu — Nature
Pollen Kiss

Dawn L. Awad   Travel
Central Park

Tashika S. Forde   Children
Julien

K. Yodice   Children
No Socks, Please!

Jose Jimenez   Nature
Night In Break

Kate M. Adams   Nature
Tread Softly

Dale F. Fifield   Nature
Holden Beach, NC

Mariea R. May   Children
What Can We Do Next

Stephanie Duncan   Children
Think Beyond

John C. Stachl   Children
Feels So Good

Keam-Mar Lai   Animals/Pets
Bagheera In Jungle

Jennifer Feldheim   Travel
Scotland

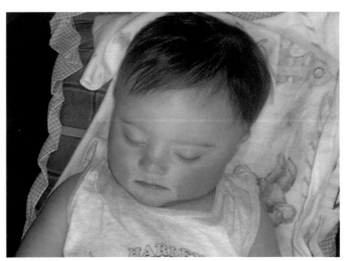

Robert J. Cordier   Children
Ethan Child

Randy Smith   Travel
Point Loma Lighthouse

Jacob Novak   Nature
Fall Fungus

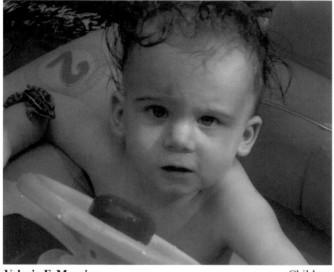

Valerie F. Mensing   Children
Carter And Frog

Cynthia Lazo   Children
Mijo

Laura Waters   Children
Jessica And The Ballet Train

Mary K. Ward   Animals/Pets
On Duty

Robyn Gibney   Animals/Pets
Pretty In Pink

Alene Corley   Travel
Looking Through A Keyhole

Mario Agostinho   Nature
The Monarch

Nancy Ward   Animals/Pets
Cheese!

Reginald W. Cason   Nature
This Beautiful White Rose

Roger Robertson   Other
Front Range Tornado

Sarah Cearley   Nature
Untitled

Travis J. Karpak   Sports
Night Game

Betty D. Davenport   Children
Private Pool

Harriette Ballard   Animals/Pets
You Mean I Have To Get Up!

Alden Bradley   Portraiture
Mom And Sis

Lindsey R. Vitale   Portraiture
Seeing It Through The Poor Man's Vision

Dorothy Cordova   Sports
Eighty-One, Still Playing Softball

Patsy Lynn Ferraro   Animals/Pets
Ernest Hemingway

Helen Dobson   Animals/Pets
Buffalo Dusting

Connie Meehyung Gledhill   Humor
Feet

Kristin Koran   Nature
Rocky Mountain Highway

Jennifer Jenkins   People
The Blues

Leona M. Rosenthal   Children
Oh, To Enjoy As A Child

Rios Diego   Other
Adventure In NY

Cathy LaGreca   Children
The Red, White, And Blue

Cristina Marie Adler   Nature
Afternoon Flowers

Michael O. Miller   Other
Eyes

Matt Michael Wilson   Other
Untitled

Jack E. Coyle　　　　　　　　　　　Nature
Reflections Of Mt. Moran

Tracy Anne Killen　　　　　　　　Animals/Pets
A Good Start

Rachael Margaret DeLoach　　　　Animals/Pets
Skipper Lakeside

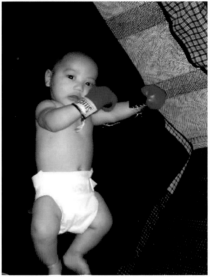

Edwin Ticne　　　　　　　　　　　Children
My First Pro Fight!

James Edward Sardonia　　　　　　Other
Standing Tall

Eleanor Leen　　　　　　　　　　　Nature
Gold In Bloom

Leona M. Rosenthal　　　　　　　　　Nature
Beauty Of The Deep

Yoly Acosta　　　　　　　　　Sports
Go Titans!

Albert David Treiber　　　　　　　　　Other
Helo Sunset

Terry Willard　　　　　　　　　Travel
Tree

Jody James　　　　　　　　　Animals/Pets
Up High

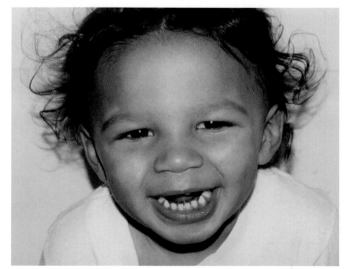

Taris Ann Neal　　　　　　　　　Children
A Child's Smile

Mikel Ortiz de Lataburu   Children
Niño Jugando En La Entrada De La Casa De Fresa Y Chocolate

Gregory Allen Boeshans   Children
Cody Bug

David W. Doty   Nature
New Hampshire Blues

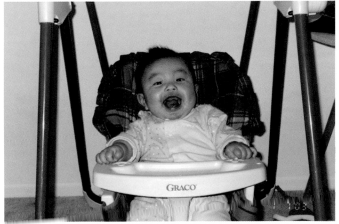

Megumi Imori   Children
No Teeth

Jon Tracy   Travel
A Pitts Sunset

Mercedes Lynn Wagner   Children
Summer Beauty

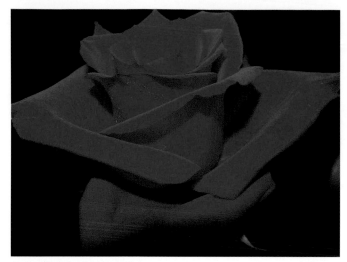

Steve Robert Limbaugh   Nature
Single Rose

Jonathan Scott   Animals/Pets
Ladybug

Kristi Waller   Children
Summer Splash!

Dana E. Foreman   Portraiture
Sunset With Missing Shadows

George M. Dorantes   Travel
Remember The Alamo

Danielle Breteau   Children
Cameron The Muffin Man

Neil Anderson Other
Crane Arrival

Judith Lynn Pratt Nature
Untitled

Joseph Franklin Fitzgerald Animals/Pets
Western Diamondback

Marilyn K. Hamilton Animals/Pets
Beautiful BamBam

Irene P. Leyson Animals/Pets
Stretching With Your Best Friend

Judy L. Herrick Children
My Boys

Tammy Lynn Pitts   Nature
Maine Morning

Kathryn Elizabeth Lapointe   Animals/Pets
Pure Comfort

Ted Boyer   Children
Got Mail

Traci R. Dubois   Children
My Little Peanut

John F. Eckrode   Humor
Swimming Car

Torbjorg Hjelmevoll-Silsby   Nature
Allegany Park, State Forest In New York

Beth Ann Rich   Children
A Day At The Beach

Rose Liston   Children
Untitled

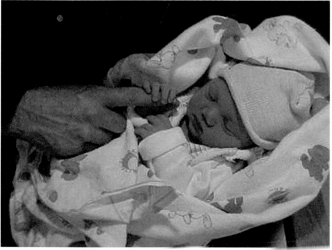

Jennifer L. Arnold   Children
Newborn Holding Daddy's Finger

Heidi Elizabeth Petersen   Children
Pure Illumination

Juan M. Melendez   Animals/Pets
Baby

Leslie Millay Thompson   Nature
Reflections

Suzanne Jackson Smith   Animals/Pets
Hollywood

Lorraine Kae Webber   Animals/Pets
Man & Dog Floating

Lisa M. Endres   Nature
Beauty Of Fishing

Dee-Ann Miles   Children
Pretty As A Princess

Patrick John Kellam   Action
Mother's Day House Fire

Charles Carpenter   Nature
Snow Falls

Katelyn Rose Ruplin Children
Innocence

Michelle F. Ortiz Nature
Ethereal Waterfall

Jeanette L. Weaver Children
Me And My Teddy

Lisa Bridget Burke Children
I Reflected Upon This Moment At The Tender Age Of 10 Months

Julian Leek Humor
Payday In Florida

Isabelle Dominique De Backer Children
Smiling Baby

Judy A. Casper   Travel
Kayaking Palau

Michelle Rae Book   Children
Dustin

Elizabeth Ann Bush   Children
Children Under The Sun

Sandra Persch   Nature
End Of The Road

James M. Green   Animals/Pets
Please Mom

Amer W. Ahmed   Nature
Perfect End To A Beautiful Day: Potomac River, Washington D.C.

Maria Faye Jones   Nature
Morning Of

Joyce Ann Smith   Children
Aloha

Wendy Ann DeLigio   People
Disturbing

Charles E. Henry Jr.   Travel
Truck On A Bridge, Savannah, GA

Michael Wayne Seale   People
Mom And Baby

Guy Vuckovic   Sports
Over The Falls

Karen Sumpter   Children
Make A Wish!

Cristina Guzman   People
David

Victor Joseph Kavy   Children
Ethan

Bev M. Mitchell   Animals/Pets
Dried Zander

Dustin Spillman   People
Compassionate Friends

Roland Matus   People
Meditation

Monica Sherman   Travel
Postcard, Anyone?

Theresa E. O'Connell   People
I'm Here

Darleen Lynde   Animals/Pets
Mama & Baby

Kristen L. Miller   Animals/Pets
Jaz Swimmimg

Heidi L. Pepin   Nature
The Sweet Nectar Of Life

Robert Lester Blalock   Action
2 p.m. Train

Monica Sulik   Portraiture
Most Content

Patricia Nell Bishop   Children
Wonder Why Mom Put A Book Titled It's Potty Time In My Bag?

Brandy Danielle Roberts   Nature
Fly On A Flower

Deborah Jean Cannaby   Children
Mr. Malachi

Brian W. Gerber   Animals/Pets
Big Bird

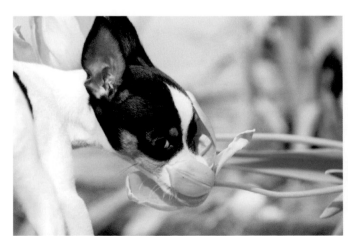

Mary Miskow   Animals/Pets
Take Time . . .

Margo M. Hatcher   Animals/Pets
Just Relaxing

Vicky King   Animals/Pets
Perfect Imperfection

Terry Lynne Dempsey   People
Child Of The Corn

Kenna Chanoux   People
Beautiful Moment

Edmilson Afonso   People
Untitled

Kathy Malecki   Other
New Friends

Tabitha Lillie Giordano   Nature
Coconut On The Beach

Toni Michelle Stamper   Nature
Purple Passion

Meri Williams   People
Cade & Granddad

Bryanne D. Willis   Nature
Morning Deer!

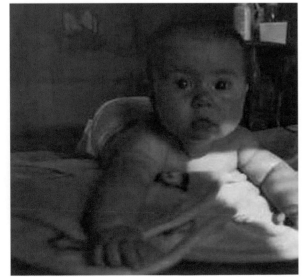

Jennifer Ann Bair   Children
Just Hanging Out

Lori L. Denney   Nature
A Bird In One Hand

James Patrick Donnelly   Children
Catch That Bird

Keri E. McMahon   Nature
Arousing Storm

Michael R. Farley   Nature
Pit Stop

Elise Ann Sumpter   Animals/Pets
My Best Friend

Terri-Lynn Catanzaro   Nature
God's Work

Enric Corbeil   Action
Lazarus, Defensive Stance

Sandra L. Banfalvy Children
If I Were Twins

Scott Myron Husted Children
Spiderweb

Toy Gerard Flores Children
Pooped!

Anna C. Wroten Other
Fenway Park, Boston

Amanda Rae Killeen Children
Ha, Mom, Did You Really Think My Legs Could Bend Like That?

Theresa Stebner Nature
Untitled

Michael Colligon   Nature
Summer Colors

Maria A. Manno   Children
Sweet And Sour

Megan Celeste Wesney   Animals/Pets
Guardian

Terry W. Hall   Animals/Pets
Mack And Janie

M. Orth   Children
Untitled

Heidi L. Clark   Children
Little Boy In Blue

Heidi Pepin   People
Proud Sisters

Steve Hallett   Other
Starburst

John Gomez   Animals/Pets
Young Hippos In Love

Nadine May Lewis   Animals/Pets
Camel Lineup

Diane A. Hughes   Animals/Pets
Curious Friends

Corinna Creedon   Action
Daddy, Look, It Is SpongeBob, What A Great Day For A Parade

Erin Reilly People
The Bride

Tim J. Short Other
Ice

Pat Frazier Animals/Pets
Little Man And Friend

Crystal Smith Children
Just Too Cute!

Brian Kurzeja Travel
Camping Trip 63

Lynne Kaye Kramer Nature
Nature's Beauty

Prashanth Arni   Other
My Future Office

Derrick Gerodd Jackson   People
Self-Portrait In Mailbox

Shawn James Martin   Portraiture
Magical Me

Eric A. Long   Other
Sunset Over Staten Island's Dump

Gwen Flanders   Children
Ben's Rosy Cheeks

Melissa Radomski   Children
Caroline Ann, Second Month

Carol Jordan   Children
Enjoying Summer In The Boston Harbor Public Water Fountain

Jayne Podesta   Nature
Stormy Weather

Karen R. Curtice   Animals/Pets
Total Surprise

Edward Friedebert Rosenthal   Children
Aymara Children

Maxine Clevenger   Animals/Pets
Untitled

Tammy Moore   Children
Cadie In High Chair

Dawn Curran Children
Cassandra Ann Curran

Becca E. Daniels People
Emily

Rebekah Jayne Edmonds Travel
Moeraki Boulders: The First One

Leanne Moore Children
Handsome

Dyana Marie Bolt Nature
Mirrored Image

Catherine Persha Children
Bath Time

Kathy Prittie Children
Snow Angels

Cathy Williams Animals/Pets
Too Much Fun For One Bichon!

Michael Colantuoni Portraiture
Precious

Beth Ann Stafford Animals/Pets
Say Cheese

Jan Darr Nature
Grand Saguaro With Mt. Lemon In The Background

Dorothy E. Burgess Nature
Snow Scene

Jason Christopher Albertson   Nature
Skyerworks

David Pyn   Children
Destiny: Eleven Weeks

Elizabeth Gray Regueira   Children
Ellie

Stacie S. Rhodes   Nature
Morning Diving

Sharon Wuehler   Nature
Message In A Bottle

Shaina Berkowitz   Travel
Approaching Early Evening Storm In Arches National Park

David Cieplechowicz   Nature
Sky Fly

Luca Boero   Animals/Pets
Mountain Gorilla In Bwindi, Uganda

Christopher Robert Brown   Nature
Stairway To Heaven

Natalie Olivia Maki   Children
Angel Eyes

Rob Gene Boertlein   Nature
Branching Out

Nancy L. Carter   Animals/Pets
Baron

Ellen Scurry Reynolds　　　　　　　Nature
Irises

Matt Sturlaugson　　　　　　　Children
Loving Hands

Vicky D. Coerper　　　　　　　Children
Kaylee

Brandon William Flaada　　　　　　　Animals/Pets
Are You Done Yet?

Wendy Elizabeth Lackner　　　　　　　Nature
Sunset On Lake Kennebec

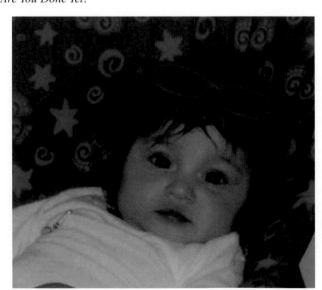

Maysaa Karkmaz　　　　　　　Children
My Angel

Paula M. Peterson   Animals/Pets
Best Friends

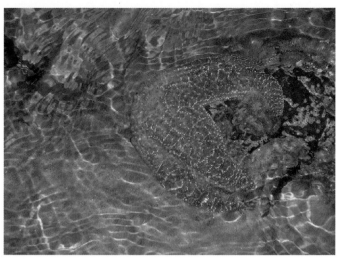

Kitty W. Turner   Nature
Pacific Ocean Starfish

Catherine Salas   Children
The Next Santa

Tas Mansuri   Action
Aliya With Attitude At Six Months!

Barbara Ellen Christ   People
Timeless Moment

Mary Frances Bush   Travel
Meigs Co., OH, Bicentennial Barn

Lori Thompson   Humor
Nap Time With Daddy

Jessica Tapia   People
Wedding Day

Melissa Ann   People
First Lady & Her Boys

Mary Elizabeth Tello   Travel
Bright Lights, Big City

Margaret Peterson   Children
Honk Honk

Russel Willard Stabler   Animals/Pets
Gregory

Leanne R. Spaulding   Animals/Pets
Scooter Playing Ball

Shay Ann Conner   Animals/Pets
Did Someone Say Bull?

Michael Dean Grabowski   Other
Alone At Sunset

Betsy Hale   Nature
The Angel After The Storm

Matthew Charles Niemuth   Nature
Sunrise Taken On December 13, 2003 Near Waupaca, Wisconsin

Jennifer Carol Owens   Animals/Pets
Lazy In The Sun

Pauline Nan O'Reilly   Animals/Pets
In My Hands

Cristina Mendez   Children
Cute As A Button

Timothy Allen Blackmon   Travel
River Crossing

Maureen McIlhenny   Children
Happy New Year!

Kim Wagner   Travel
Dublin Mountains, Ireland

Jeanna M. Hunt-Rattenborg   Other
Rusted And Abandoned

Terry W. Ragsdale   Travel
Paris At Night

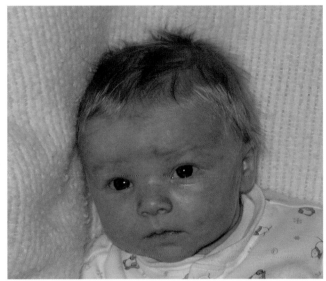

Diana J. Cline   Animals/Pets
A Closer Look

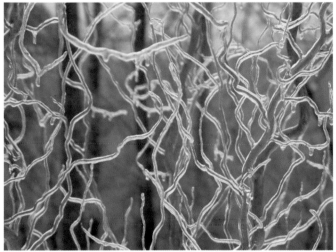

Kristi Monet   Nature
Iced Willow

Lori Anne Marshall   Children
Innocence

Mary Jo Sheppard   Nature
Hilton Head Rain Forest

Kristy Lee Varunan   Children
Flower Girl

David A. Crumb   Animals/Pets
Sci-Fi Sleeps

Dannette Marie Longo   Nature
Tranquility

Tatyana Shkop   Travel
Crimea, Ukraine, 2004: That Rock Named Diva . . .

Punit Baxi   Travel
Pleasant Evening After Snowfall

Becky Aguillard   Children
Nicholas Learning To Crawl

Doreen Vitkuske-Blumberg   Children
Tub Time

Kimberly Sutton   Nature
Buzzing Around My Garden

Adrienne Solloway   Children
Cheyenne

Mark Ramelb   People
Malia & Mike, November 27, 2004

Mick L. Finley   Nature
Yesterday

Janice Schlenvogt   Animals/Pets
Sophie In Her Stroller!

Leonie E. Schroer   Nature
Lotus

Cheri Lisa Pascual   Nature
Hummingbird

Erin Higby   Other
L' Innocenza

Nikohl Lynn Urban   Animals/Pets
Shy Puppy

Brenna Nicole Zumbro   Nature
Newgrange

Christina Sierra   Children
Potty Help

Mariko Grace Erekson   Other
Island Life

Sudhir Raghavan — Nature
Beautiful Life: Upside Down Or Downside Up!

Amy Darlene Chrysler — Children
Two Pumpkins

Jake Ty Carver — Animals/Pets
Frolic In The Snow

Eva Leone Zreczycki — Nature
Blue Heart

June Holoch — Travel
Sailboat In Mexico

Ming Ming Beh — People
A Girl With A Mask

Carolyn S. Hart   Children
Yum Yum

Rick Long   Nature
A Moment In Time

Yan Guo   Nature
Autumn Sky

Nicole A. Franc   Nature
Sunset Solo

Robert Shane Postma   Nature
Fire In The Sky

Charles Lagana   Travel
Statue Of Liberty

Dennis Borovy Travel
Vacation In Maine!

Nancy C. Kling Animals/Pets
Pride

Emily A. Drake Nature
White Mountains

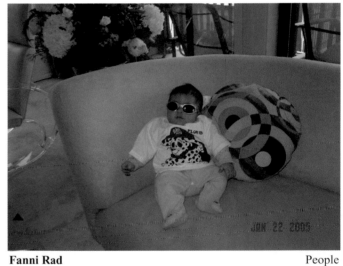

Fanni Rad People
My First Sunglasses

Nadya Nemova Tatsch Children
Me And My Baby

Maria Tanya de Guzman Viera People
My Greatest Love For Malachi

91

Darion Andrew Quarles People
Here's Looking At You, Kid

Julie Baier Children
What A Beautiful World We Live In (La Jolla, CA)

Ian Phillip Aizman Nature
Gentle Blossom

Hsiao Ying Huang Children
Princess Snow White And Me

Tyler Moore Children
J.T. Moore: Ladies Man At One Week!

Deedra Nell Marleen Wolski Animals/Pets
Kanned Kitty

Karen Y. Lewellyn   Children
First Time Holding A Leaf

Andrea Faris Roberts   Children
In Heaven's Light

Jayne Beatty   Sports
Holding On By A Hair!

Gregg Allan Biedler   Animals/Pets
Gorilla In The Snow

Wanda Katherine Baker   Children
Look At Me

Dawn Marie Frost   Humor
Water Babies Part II

Holli Goering — Children
Wyatt & Bunny Baby On A Summer Day Enjoying The Outdoors

Lynda Jennings — Children
Good Sport

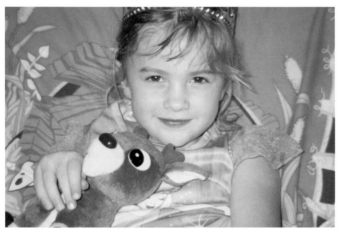

Wendy Siepler — Humor
Momma, Can We Have Christmas Again Today?

Jennifer Allen — Children
Pumpkin Patch

Kara LaPres — Animals/Pets
Pouting

Jaime Deborah Dunnavant — Nature
Silver Lining

Terri Bramley   Children
Summer Fun

Jason Scott Bragdon   People
A Mother's Prayer

Larry Vipond   Portraiture
Senior Elegance

Carol L. Antonio   Other
Bubble-osity

Pooya Ebrahim   People
Eye

Shannon B. Urban   Children
Exhilaration!

Amanda Ann Jones   Children
Skipping Rope

Kathie Doran   Other
Kate

Kathleen Armstrong   Children
My Little Pumpkin

Jamie Plaster   People
Mommy And Her Baby Girl

Tina Lacugnato   Nature
Go With The Flow

Sati Oda   Animals/Pets
A Puppy On The Beach

Robert Poe — Animals/Pets
Two Does

Velmar Pewee Hale Johnson — Children
Who Called My Name?

Janet L. Young — Travel
Fine Art Of Narita

Eric Hull — Children
Do I Know You?

Olivia Hardison — Travel
Future Fireman

John Carrick Turner — Nature
Sun Dogs & Ice Crystals

Robert Tella   People
Little Girl

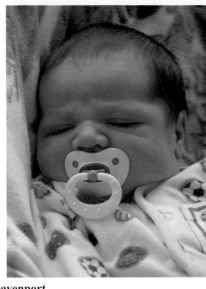

Bethany Davenport   Children
Peaceful Dreams

Brendan Hegwood   Animals/Pets
Stare Down

Shai M. Schryver   Nature
Between Night And Day

Brooke Fonseca   Children
I Did It!

Amy B. Hogan   Children
I Love You!

Franƴoise Egger Animals/Pets
Naze Napping

Joseph Philip Clarke Animals/Pets
Good Boy

Stacey Elizabeth Morse Children
A Musician In The Making

Melinda Laura Byrd People
Jack In Hat

Peggy Harrison Children
Smelling The Roses!

Beth Ann Noferi Portraiture
Portrait Of Lee

Aldela C. Jackson   Children
Sleeping On My Basket

Peggy L. Grieme   Children
Who's That Cutie In The Mirror!

Richel Leslie Stephenson   People
Bless This Baby

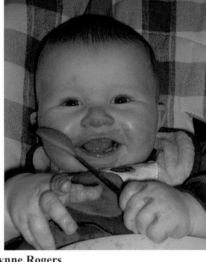

Deborah Lynne Rogers   Children
Sean Enjoying Dinner

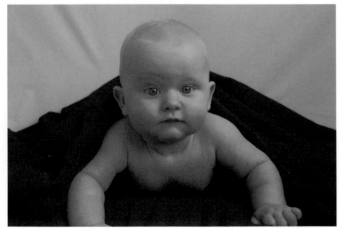

Dorothy Jasinski   Children
Be My Valentine

Beth Anne Wile   Nature
Sweet Dreams

Damon Sean Cowart   Portraiture
The Man In The Hat

Mary Kathryn High   Animals/Pets
Ducks On The Pond

Casey Graham   Travel
Popham Beach

Lissa Hudson Measel   Children
Going To The Beach

Cory Samillano   Sports
Super Bowl XXXIX Fireworks

Jeremy Price   Children
This Way Up

Guy Levin Travel
Reign Of The Inca

Ada Juntunen Children
Pure Joy In The Eyes Of A Child

Youngsook An Children
I Am A Boy Now

Sean Patrick Sullivan Nature
Mule Ears, Big Bend National Park, TX

Lisa Fusaro Children
Little Mermaids

Darren J. Flynn Children
Victoria

Christina Marie Wnek   Children
Don't Mess With Me, Mom

Andrew Gibson   Animals/Pets
Cave Rabbit

Andrew Johnson   Travel
Another Afternoon

Chanti Berube   People
Push Me, Push Me: Great-Grands Mami & Falon

Gregory Toussaint   Nature
Buttermilk Falls

Daniela Palafax   Children
Chillin' In The Crib

Ken Melnikoff   Humor
Halloween Surprise

Rainy Elisabeth Whitehill   Children
Sweet Baby

Renata Abdo   Travel
Praia Do Forte, BA, Brazil

Brandy S. Missroon   Children
My Valentine In Vermont

John Paul Sard Jr.   Nature
Lightning On The Choptank

Maribel R. Robles   Nature
Roatan, Honduras

Joseph P. Grano Travel
Lonely View

Thomas A. Wood Travel
Gettysburg Sunset

Shannen Marie Moore Other
Shannen And Yogi

Shannon Lee Jordan Children
The Real Baby Jordan Lee

Richard Patterson Nature
Sierra Peak

Stacie J. Leavitt Children
My Prince

Eddie Hopkins　　　　　　　　　　　　　　　　　Humor
Matador Randy

Melinda Kerstetter　　　　　　　　　　　　　　Children
Noah's Christmas Candy Lane

Ridgely Myers　　　　　　　　　　　　　　　　　Action
Crazy Connor

Diana Cozzens　　　　　　　　　　　　　　　　　Nature
Deer At Sequoia National Park

Krista Furtney　　　　　　　　　　　　　　　　　People
Happy Baby!

Jamie Harkins　　　　　　　　　　　　　　　Animals/Pets
Under The Sea . . .

Chrissy Elia Portraiture
Ape

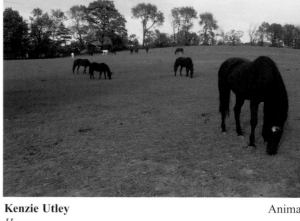

Kenzie Utley Animals/Pets
Horses

Camille Saka Children
If I Could Read Your Mind . . .

Rogelio Hernandez Children
Bundled Up

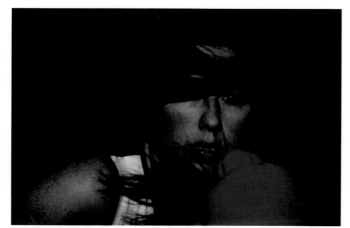

Katarzyna Cichowicz People
Inside Me

Michelle Jean Poole Children
The Gate Escape For Ethan

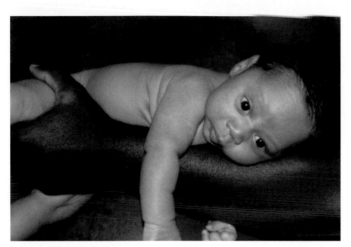

Tamara Renee Arhin   Children
In Dad's Arms

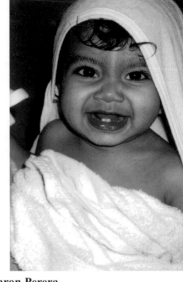

Marietta Sharon Perera   Children
Feeling Fresh!

Sherri E. Wiggins   Children
Safe In Dad's Arms

Anthony F. Lacey   Animals/Pets
Making Friends

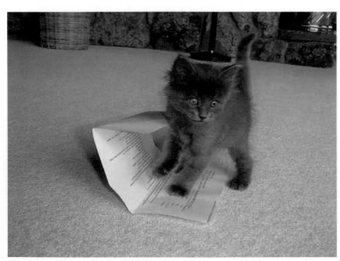

Judith A. Nichol   Animals/Pets
Snuggles

Christine Manchester   Children
Peekaboo!

J. Okin People
BJ's Carpentry At Best

Sheila Erickson Children
So Happy To Be Flower Girl

Samantha Vargo People
Loving Leaves

Tara Funair Children
My Little Santa

Sandra Grout Children
Best Friends

Karen Harrington Children
Already Extreme Rock Climbing At Two-And-A-Half!

Cathy Lynn Lanham   Nature
At Day's End

Kirk Wright   Nature
Floating

Kathy J. Ingalls   Other
Sunset In Ohio

Ellen McGarigal   Animals/Pets
Deer Outside My Kitchen Window

Erin Kathleen Clark   Children
Precious Eyes

Ana Easlick   Children
Holiday Magic

Lisa Hirai — Children
Sammy

F. Daniel Leach — Children
Daniel In Bouncy Seat

Kamila Milewska — Children
Joy Of Life

Terri Pham — Portraiture
My Best Friend Glows

Angela Schol — Animals/Pets
Alexander's First Christmas

Darla Maynard — Travel
Look Ma, No Hands . . . Yeah Right!

Stacey Smith
Race Day

Sports

Patty Hicks
Patty's Little Chatter

Animals/Pets

Kelly Moyer
Pot Of Smiles

Children

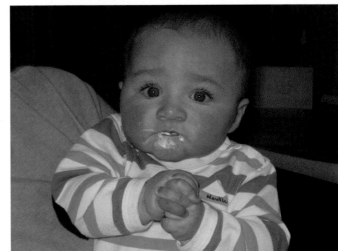

Nikki Kenoyer
Yummy Cake

Children

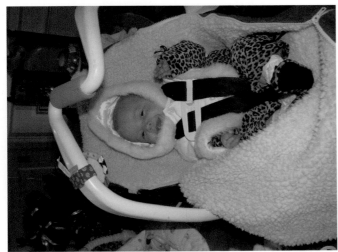

Sarah Leclaire
Hello Kitty

Children

Kristen Foley
Snoozin'

Children

Wesley Joe Landrum — Animals/Pets
Ready For Takeoff

Tina Marie Chaidez — People
Captured

Ted Homjak — Nature
Dominant Bull

Robert Vega — Travel
The Limestone Walls Of El Morro

Shalyn M. Orange — Animals/Pets
Princess Boots

Stacy Green — Humor
Hungry Hippo

Matthew P. Cohen   Humor
Puppy Love

Monica Freyre   Children
Chili Pepper Baby

Erin Fagan   Children
The Innocence Of Fall

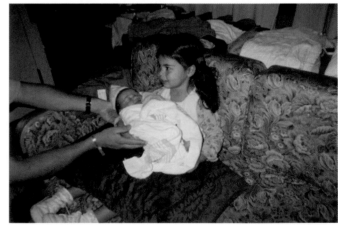

Brenda Yeatman   Children
Zoe Meets Gia

Kao Xu Chang   Children
Starfish Anyone?

Sheryl Marie Schmidt   Portraiture
Eurasian Owl

Robert B. Norton Travel
Nantucket Harbor, January 2004

Stephen R. Franklin Nature
Beyond The Realms

Wayne Dudley Other
Fractured Light

Cathy Gyselbrecht Children
Fearless Flyer

Jody Perdomo Nature
Melting Quick

Tereasa D. McCoy Nature
Nature

Layla Haddox   Animals/Pets
Salem

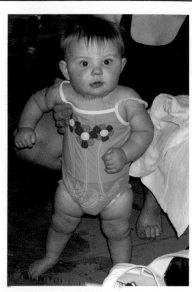

Penny Reinders   Children
Dylann And Her Thighs

Angelica MacFarland   Travel
Sunset Beach Bridge

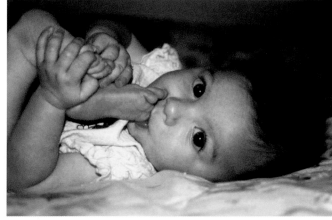

Dawn Aye   Children
Lea

Lisa Mastalier   Children
Zachary Yearns

Marixa Pena   Nature
Barcelona On Fire!

John Walter Hawkins   Travel
Main Street: Cumberland, MD

Stephanie Long   People
Our Miracle

Duke W, Heaton   Nature
Reflection

Elizabeth Hobbs   Sports
Last Hole

Doris Haworth   Children
Charlie The Cabbage Patch Kid

Jan Knop   Portraiture
Winter In Greenwich Village

Sue Meredith Nature
Highland Park Butterfly, Rochester, New York

Grace Marie Estes Children
My Little Angel

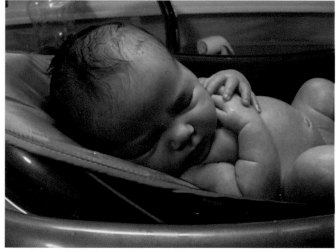

Diana Ladd Wilson Children
Blissful Bathing

Lisa Tuggle Nature
Summer Flower

Nikki Renee Youso Portraiture
Serenity

Daniella Vitolo Children
Alexandra, 4 1/2 Months Old, Is Picking Out A Tangerine

Linda Wahaski Children

I Have Everything A Boy Could Ever Want: Love And Toys!

Debbie Vanderhoef Animals/Pets

Ziggy's First Snow

Peilan Johnson Children

I See You

Jason Ostrander Nature

Pax Vobiscum

Pam Rehbein Animals/Pets

Will Someone Please Be My Valentine?

Lorraine G. King Animals/Pets

The Dogs Are Enjoyed

Tonya Lenette Freeman Children
Too Cute

Barbara Burgess Children
Gardening Girls

Jonathan Fitzgerald Kay Nature
A Little Sun

Levi Silva Children
Maile Playing Hide-And-Seek

Anita Amidon Children
Here I Am!

Annie Taliaferro Nature
Zen Waterfall

Ramona Rogers   Nature
How Cute

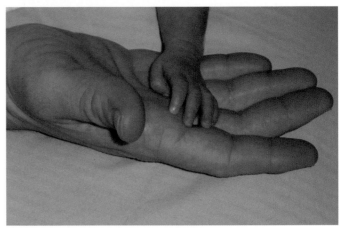

Karen Maw   Children
In Daddy's Hand

Benny Pontiveros   Travel
Taytay Waterfalls, Majayjay, Laguna, Philippines

Maricar Bolante   Animals/Pets
Max

Pamela Dupuis   Children
Zachary Dupuis

Jeri Krause   Travel
Come Inside

Kristin Cole   Animals/Pets
Brotherly Love

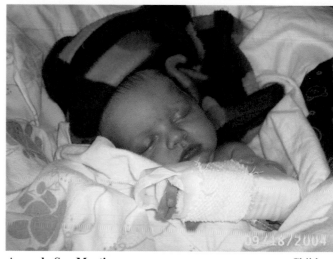

Amanda Sue Martinez   Children
Sweet Baby

Lora Collins   Animals/Pets
Spaz On His Throne

Janet Graber   Nature
Mountains Reflections

Pam Hoffee   Travel
Sand

Dixie Todd   Nature
Lighting The Way

Teresa Harris   Other
A Full Load

Mary Busti   Nature
Reflections Of Autumn

Suzanne G. Brochu   Nature
VT Tree Determined To Grow

Becky Chatwin   Children
Believe

Nancy E. Roberts   Sports
The Will To Win

Delinda Gaona   Nature
Amanecer

Denise Volturo   Children
Kissing Twins

Del A. Krumbein   Animals/Pets
Corgi, R & R (Relaxing And Reading)

Tisha Holmes   Children
Little Reader

Apryle B. Smart   Travel
Forever Changed

Jeannie Douglas-Sevier   Children
Slide Time

Carla Salera   Sports
Boogie Boardin'

Jane Arendsen   Nature
Icy Lights

Robert Williams   Animals/Pets
Mister Pete

Susan Neves   Humor
Who Is Going To Tell Mom?

Michelle L. McCall   Nature
The Mighty Tiger

Carolyn Salsgiver   Nature
Down Winter Lane

V. Jeanne Girovasi   Nature
Help, I Fell In And Can't Get Out

Arturo R. Loayza Nature
Frog On Tree Stump

Andrea Larkins Children
Pleasing Mother

Regina Bay Other
American Dream

Vera Mickelboro Nature
Winter Beauty

Casey Kaldenberg Nature
Winter Sky

Sharon Finney Nature
Old Railroad Bridge, Elgin, KS

Cynthiann Shaw　　　　　　　　　Nature
Infrared Photo Of Park, 2003

Martha Kautz　　　　　　　　　Nature
Serene Serendipity

Karen Nicolls　　　　　　　　　Nature
Quiet Moments

Russ Davenport　　　　　　　　　Nature
Ripples In Color

Todd Smith　　　　　　　　　Travel
The West Rim Road

Inge K. Molzahn　　　　　　　　　Nature
Ragged Point, California

Faith Hoffman   Nature
Swans Nesting Within City Limits

Colleen E. Moore   People
Anticipation

Shanelle Weaver   Travel
Brejo Santo, Brazil

Lynne Munger   Animals/Pets
Val In Dandelions

Amanda Moye   Nature
Sweet Georgia Morn

Christy Saetern   Animals/Pets
Ahh . . . The Great Outdoors

Candice Hinshaw   Animals/Pets
Dunken's Desire

Donovon D. Mason   People
School Children On "School Bus," Shanghai Zoo, 1983

Debbie Kiesel   Nature
Hummingbird At Dinner

Juan Marcelo Tapari   People
Forever In My Heart

Lisa L. Davis   Animals/Pets
You Are My Sunshine (Sunny D)

Benjamin Casimir Mack   People
The Five Men Of Corleone (I Cinque Yomini Di Corleone)

Jarrod Smith   Nature
A Mother's Devotion

Bonnie Aldrich   People
Things Change

Sicily Gargano   Other
Where?

Anthony May   Nature
Jamaican Flower

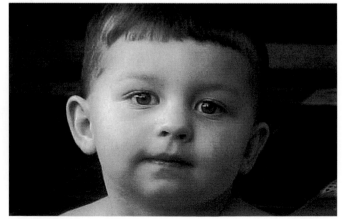

Laura Sheridan   Children
Ryan

Chuck Schmiedlin   Animals/Pets
Mocha Gaze

Deanna Ruble   Portraiture
Miracle From God

Dana Green   People
Love At First Sight

Joseph A. Stumpf III   Other
City's Peace

Anna Wu   Other
Playground Vendor's Stand

Brenda Lanier   Children
The Wink

Tammera J. Alliss   Nature
Rosemary

Aaron Graves   Portraiture
Vanessa

Patrick Haggerty   Nature
Iris

Lowell R. Schrupp   Action
Good-Bye Columbia

Michelle Landis   Nature
Under The Boardwalk

Jennie Crist   Nature
Nesting Killdeer

Jennifer Sorensen   Nature
Ice Houses On Hall Lake

Marcia A. Bordovsky Children
Bordovskys In Bluebonnets

Carol A. Ward Nature
Fish, Fish, Fish

Susan Burkhart Nature
Winter In A Box

Hai Vo Animals/Pets
Delicious Meal

Jean Hunt Nature
Sunset At Jekyll Island

Barbara Thompson Animals/Pets
White Ibis Munching At Silver Key, Sanibel, Florida

Julia Dvoskina Children
Child's Play

Linda Thornton Animals/Pets
Camouflage Or Illusion

Lisa Becker Children
Untitled

Betty Allen Nature
A Christmas Angel

Abby Munoz Other
Forgotten Childhood

Justin Whisenant Nature
Dusk Till Dawn

John Fitzgerald   Other
Avg Scramble 1941

Carmen Estelle Wilson   Children
Intense Love

Jonathan Lane   Travel
Cambodian Doorway

Tracey Salmo   Children
I Promised You The Moon

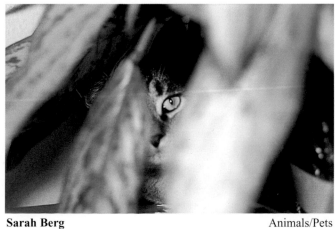

Sarah Berg   Animals/Pets
Tigger

Carrie Pospishil   Other
A Century Ago: Dakota Historical Home

Barbara Childress Animals/Pets
Wanna Shoot Hoops?

Austin Wood Children
My Son

Hionia Konev Nature
The Million Dollar View

Kim R. Adams Children
Queen Of The Jungle

Beth Powers Children
I Love My Mommy!

Erika Zielinski Nature
Untitled

Yvette Grem Animals/Pets
Stuck In The Bucket

Daniel A. Smith Nature
Busy Bee

Lesley S. M. Hutchinson People
Dante In Denim Duds

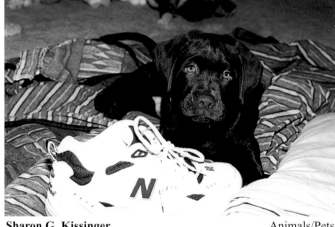

Sharon G. Kissinger Animals/Pets
Untitled

Roberta Jay Lindquist Children
October Giraffe

Evelyn Fulweiler Nature
Winter Sunrise

Bobby Ray Worley   Children
Best Buddies

Shirley Schneider   Nature
Winter Magic

Carmen A. Sexton   People
Endless Love

Lorraine Green   Children
Baby Brother

Terry L. Baylor   Nature
Ice On The Beach

Betty Gentry   Nature
The Beginning

Lacy Woods   Animals/Pets
Patiently Waiting

Jennifer Palesotti   Children
A Pure Jewel

Paige Hutchison   Travel
Reflections

Keni Taylor   Animals/Pets
Dog Pack

Verna McNatt   Travel
Sunset, Inside Passage

Erica Jon Emanuel   Nature
Eagle Lake, Desolation Wilderness

Frances Goldworthy   Children
Dreaming

Jacqueline Palmer   Children
A Moment To Reflect

Belinda Doyle   People
Subliminal

Chris Strauss   Travel
Key West Sunset

Lee R. Mills   Travel
Ore Wagon In Bode, California (What Was It Like Back Then?)

Shirley May Pyle   Nature
Fine Feathered Friend

Paul Jones People
Pride

Stacey M. Gifford Animals/Pets
Tiny Penguin

Casey Whiteaker Animals/Pets
Serenity

Olga Baer Animals/Pets
Tiger

Crystal Pollock Other
Birds

Todd M. Smith Children
First Time Afloat

Charlene Vaughn
Monarch Of The Garden

Nature

Kim Rehm
Lake Ontario Sunset

Nature

Linda F. Harkins
"Miyako Odori" In Gion, Kyoto

Travel

Eleanor Macey
Aruba Arch

Nature

Jane Eustice
First Limo Ride

Children

Patricia Dascomb
Well, It's A Clown's World

Children

Aimee Ellis People
Cinderella Story

Kim Horan Animals/Pets
Chillin' Under Florida Sunshine

Nancy Kitchen Austin Nature
Birds

Susan Schmidt Children
Our Little Angel

Geri Ewing Children
Victory Lap

Diane Egan Portraiture
Jungle Boy

Trudy Hosking Nature
Footprints

Gabrielle Wierzbicki Nature
Euphoric Radiance

Marion Lewis Children
Expression And Feelings

Brenda Zimmerman Children
A Day In The Waves

Crystal A. Laster People
Spring Beauty

Jill Gentry Nature
Down Silver Creek Falls

Donald Whisenhunt Action
The Good Old Days

Rose Hager Nature
Sunset Magic

Olivia West Children
Victoria Rose Tapia Sitting Pretty

Mark Bosman Nature
Winter Falls

Dan Sullivan Sports
The View From The Beach

Francesca Sanderson Children
Margot Sophia Looking Elegant And Smart

Jayne Cachia
Candlelight

Children

David Byrum
Honduran Hibiscus

Nature

Pellie M. Green
Untitled

Nature

Judith Smith
The Butterfly

Nature

Stephanie Braden
Striped Beauty

Nature

Michelle Tinger
Bee's Attraction

Nature

Donna Werner   Nature
Wyoming Sunset

Edna Harris   Nature
Waterfall Pool

Jenna Wysong   Nature
Frozen In Time

Michele Voccola   Animals/Pets
Casual Canine

Maya Catron   Travel
Eiffel Tower At Night

D. Blankenschipf   Nature
Morning Butterfly

147

Donald C. Szymanski   Other
Hot Air Balloon

Melissa Allen   Children
China Doll

Roland Kuhlenbeck   Nature
Fiery Illusion

Robert D. Barnes Sr.   Nature
Gotcha

Theresa Plevny   Nature
Rivers Of Living Water

Barbara Hamuka   Nature
Nature's Rainbow Of Color

Matthew Olson   Children
Summertime Contentment

Shawna Vann   Children
Shawna's Angel

Karen L. Phillips   Animals/Pets
Buddy: A Sweet Bichon Frise

Nicole Powell   Children
Hanging Around

Jennifer Rotar   Children
Ride 'Em, Cowboy

Mitchell Smith   Nature
Spring Surprises

Echo Lynette Bunce   Nature
Rare Sky

Mark P. Anderson   Nature
Gooseberry Fawn

Gina Cook   Children
Without A Care In The World

Gina Rickey   Portraiture
Country Sunshine

Barbara O'Der   Nature
Shadows

Marge Rahnenfuehrer   Children
I Love You, You Love Me, Don't You?

Jerry Sinquefield Nature
Bent Walnut

Mikki Blackford Nature
Mystic Falls Of Bridgeton Mills

Kawao M. Tanong Nature
Hawaii Sunrise

Sue Foreman Nature
Lunch Break

Frank S. Pizzardi Other
Which Is Older?

Wanda Pogue Travel
Serenity

James Ware   Other
Foxglove

Patrick Rose   Animals/Pets
Mei Mei

Pat Barton   Nature
Black Canyon

Stacey May   Children
My First Bike

Jennifer Whyte   Other
Train From Potosi, WI Campground

Duane Heineck   Nature
The Red Beauty

Judith Young   Nature
Ending Of A Perfect Day

Hunter Owen Thompson   Nature
Frozen In Time

Gary Masters   Nature
Blue Mediterranean

Kelli Frost   Nature
A Little Peace Of Nature

Roger Bidwell   Nature
Midnight Gold

KJ Cowen   Sports
Double Take

Kris Malkoski   Children
Electrifying Ride

Heathyr Clift   People
Harnessing The Light

Ann Wong   Nature
Digitalis

Maria Daniela Sierra   Other
Aterrizage

Elizabeth Rushlow   Nature
Sunrise Over Paradise Found

Kay L. Newell   Animals/Pets
Deep Thought

154

Jennifer Siegwart   Other
90th And I

Dorothy E. Cooney   Nature
Eagle At Sunrise

Silvia Beatriz Andrade   Children
Catalina

Roberta Connolly   Animals/Pets
Feeding Time

Joan Warren   Animals/Pets
Sugar And Spice

Jennifer Blake   Children
Growing Together

Karen R. Gearhart　　　　　　　　　　Animals/Pets
Penny

Darrell Becker　　　　　　　　　　Other
Ila's House

David A. Scherer　　　　　　　　　　Nature
The Birds Have Vacated, Now It's My Turn

Jimmie Varju　　　　　　　　　　Nature
Afternoon Delight

Phil Pryde　　　　　　　　　　Nature
I Found The Place To Be

Keith Briggs　　　　　　　　　　Children
A Child's Moment In Time

Virginia Kingery   Other
Boots And Hat

Debra Dettone   Animals/Pets
Come Play With Me!

Suzanne McLean   Travel
Copenhagen

Vera Buck   Nature
Yellow Rose

Barbara Mensch   Animals/Pets
Nature's Grays

Jeremy Wisecup   Travel
A Building Within A Building

Tami Phillips Nature
Reflection Of Peace

Laura D. Szymaszek Children
Jessica And Friends

Winnie Riester Animals/Pets
Got Milk?

Judi Hoerth Animals/Pets
Is He For Real?

Cliff Williams Other
Ye Olde Grist Mill

Bob Kozma Nature
A Friendly Loon

Sara Rapuano
Solitary Blossom

Nature

Justina Gonzalez
Forever Young

Children

Deb Becker
The Boys

Animals/Pets

Sam Troutman Jr.
Flying High Finish

Sports

Nelson Garcia
La Carreta (The Cart)

Nature

Jessica Mosser
Morning Wonder

Animals/Pets

Penny Laster   Animals/Pets
Two-Day-Old Black Jack

Patricia Erickson   Portraiture
Fallin' Into Fun

Nanci Nicholas   People
Lean On Me

Kathryn A. Way   Animals/Pets
Tellin' It Like It Is

Barbara Smith   Nature
Pink Bells Ringing In Summer

Karen White   Animals/Pets
Lazy Daze

Janet Lynne Jones   Children
Oh, What A Beautiful Babe

Debbie Lester   Children
All Tuckered Out

Rod Sipes   Nature
Bird Of Paradise

Kimberly Erickson   Children
Haulin' Hay

Janet Vavra   Animals/Pets
Chicken Hen Raising Ducks

Tara F. LeBlanc   Children
Dustin Luke LeBlanc Fishing At The Camp

April Susan Reno   Children
Don't Worry, We Have Everything Under Control

Debbie Sanders   Travel
White Sands, New Mexico

Clare Kalisher   Children
Our Little Pumpkin

Richard A. King   Nature
Spring Morning Retreat

Nancy Reece   Children
Boy Meets World

Rutha S. Walker   People
My Little Logger

Lisa Piller Travel
When In Vegas

Sheri C. Hammonds Children
Nicole Going To Kiss The Baby Fawn

William J. Smith Travel
Long Day Ahead

Marilyn M. Harker Nature
The Pot Is Behind The Shed!

Judith Ann Frick Children
Innocence & Erotica, Girl On Bus, Bondi Beach, Sydney, Australia

Vicki Mayberry Children
Hayden's Hands

William C. Kohler   People
293 Years Of Sizzle

Anita A. Caudill   Portraiture
Treasured Moments

Jack Antila   Other
I'm Just A Shadow Of Myself

Martha T. Turner   Children
Kissing Cousins

Alan Hoffman   Portraiture
Latte Drinker

Polly A. Zeiner   Nature
Butterfly At Rest

Laureen Aversa   Other
Trip To D.C.

Julia M. Winfree   Animals/Pets
Frosty Tells Santa What He Wants For Christmas

Sandra Kneile   Animals/Pets
Prashanti

Branda Jones   Travel
Eiffel Tower

Dean Lodzinski   People
Let Me Sleep

Donald Urquidez   Travel
Reflections Of A Lodge

Barbara Melia   Animals/Pets
Love That Catnip!

Kimberly A. Ashley   Other
Tranquility

Deonna Hoffman   Travel
Reliving The Lewis And Clark Adventures

Leslie Gilson   Sports
Don't Worry, Swim Lessons Will Soon Be Over

Manuel Maldonado   Travel
Puerto Rico: The Door To History

April Riley   Nature
Audra State Park

Meagan Parks People
True Rednecks

Ann Greenwood Nature
Reach For The Rays

Nisha Holleman Nature
Ocean Sunset

Erin Johnson Nature
Truth

W. V. Price Sports
Don't Bother Me While I'm Fishing!

Nancy Hagan Other
Gone With The Wind

Marvin Elliott Ellis People
Papa Guede

Wendy Landers Nature
My First Watermelon

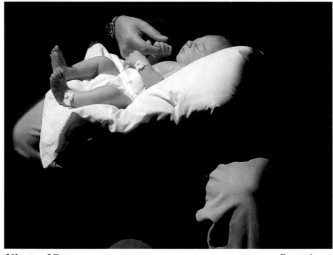

Kirsten Vignec Portraiture
Bonding With Olivia

Reita K. Scudder Animals/Pets
Emerson

Kathy Michael Children
Just Hanging Around

Laurel Furbish Action
Battlefield

Caroline Hancock   Nature
Red Lory

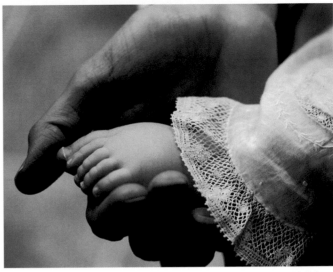

Fran Slaughter   Children
The Christening

William Carpenter   Nature
Lonely Tulip

Morayma Alonzo   Children
Sweet Child

Pierre Hamon   People
The Photographer

Kathy Everidge   Nature
Blooming Pear

Judith Molnar   Children
Just Like Dad

Jean Lappe   Animals/Pets
Special Gift

Kara Miller   Travel
Twilight Beach

Susan M. Carroll   Nature
Renewing Dew

Wayne Crump   Nature
An Early Spring Visitor

Kim Holz   Other
Bike In Shed

Naomi Viso   Sports
Changing On The Fly

Cheri Doessel   Children
Relaxing At The Beach

B. James Webster   Travel
How Do You See The Shiprock

Penelope P. Webb   Humor
Danced The Night Away

Jeff Barney   Nature
Cecropia Moths

Casandra Molina   Animals/Pets
Lake Girl

171

Dwight Hewitt   Children
Mom . . . What Do I Do Now?

Regina Armstrong   Nature
Approaching Storm

Edward D. Thayne   Nature
Feed Me, Please

Cynthia Rose McCarron   Action
Spinning Wheel

Kelly M. McCormick   Children
Kathryn

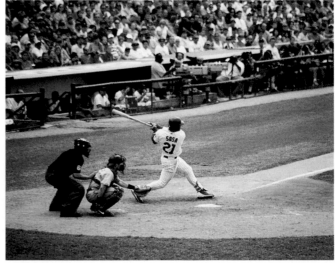

Jason Kemp   Sports
History In The Making

Dee Isle Nature
The First Snow

Judith L. Magowan Children
I See You!

Jonathan Davis Other
The Past Revisited

Sarah Durr Other
Remember When

Colleen Moritz Humor
Too Cool For Joey

Glenn Layton Nature
Here's Lookin' At Ya

Aimee Maria Meinzen   Animals/Pets
I'm Ready For My Close-Up

Ron Prieto   People
Ahh

Courtney Civis-Mesete   Children
Childhood Explorations

Scott Winans   Children
A Friend Loves At All Times

Roy Borras   Portraiture
Generation

Savannah C. Clark   People
Pigeon-Toed

Lisa Gross   People
Lady Of Corfu

Everett L. Grant Jr.   Nature
The Tennessee Southern Lights

Shari Morisset   Nature
Dusk At Crescent Lake

Robert C. Drost   Nature
Nature's Glory

Michelle E. Clegg   Nature
Springhouse

Matthew Lundy   Nature
Sunset On Chain Lake

Tenefer Scipio   People
Tourist

Adam Bulger   Other
Haunted House

Joe Rogers   People
The Last Stop

Alice Turner   Nature
Solitude

Robert Edwards   Sports
Pikes Peak Hill Climb

Julie M. Poston   Children
Dreaming Angel

Roger Dead Foster   Travel
Majestic Beauty

Robert L. Steed   Nature
Dew Caressed Plumerias

Amy Goldman   Animals/Pets
Caly

Ann James   Children
Sharing With My Sister

Marjorie Murtha Butler   Nature
The Fly And The Spider

Heather Witham   Children
Justin And Audrey, Fun On The Farm

John Brier Other
Sparklers Of The Night

Verna L. Finwick Animals/Pets
Big Mouth Lion

Terry L. DeFee Travel
Swan Covered Bridge

Faith Krause Nature
A Rare Find

Jason Arand Animals/Pets
First Glance

O. Volkmann Nature
Where's The Snow?

Melinda Carr　　　　　　　　　　　Travel
The Challenger

Margie Robinson　　　　　　　　　　Nature
Selkirk Mountains Rainbow

Bob Chance　　　　　　　　　　　Nature
Chinese Anemone

Mary Anne Jensen　　　　　　　　　Nature
Barn In Spring

Mary Montgomery　　　　　　　　　Children
Cooling Off

Jerri Rogers　　　　　　　　　　Portraiture
Dreamin' Of Ponies

Wanda Jean Fountain   Other
Let Light Shine Out Of Darkness

Sheri Harper   Nature
In Plane View

Patricia Barnett   Nature
Morning Dew

Fawn Frazer   Nature
A Wave In Time

Gaye N. Higginson   Humor
Single File, Please

Tammy Romans   Nature
Morning Stroll

Betty Pamias   Children
A Futuristic Past

Mary Jo Garvin   Animals/Pets
A Nap Interrupted

Misty Cox   Children
Baby Blues

Darlene J. Lehman   Humor
Sticking My Neck Out . . .

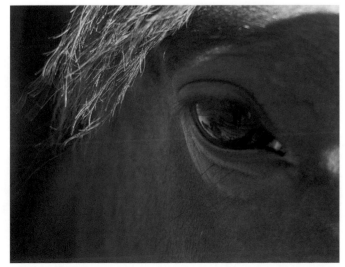

Christy Hanson   Animals/Pets
Destiny

Lindsay Jacobson   Animals/Pets
Excuse Me . . . Could You Pass The Sunblock?

Patrick Faden   Travel
Reflecting

Robert F. Duerr Jr.   Nature
Warming Her Wings

Judy R. Smith   Humor
Red River Trout

Arlene Wyman   Travel
NYC Greets Queen Mary 2

Amanda Johnson   Animals/Pets
Serene Sisters

Kimberly J. Sadowski   Nature
Reflect

Jill Valero Other
A View To Remember

Michael Lang Nature
Ocean Paradise

Tasha Garmon Nature
Reflections On The Beach

Deloris English Nature
Sweet Solitude

Attila Gulyas Animals/Pets
Follow Me . . .

Pam Vayette Nature
Catchin' Some Rays

Stacy Chandler Animals/Pets
Serenity

Heidi Fagley Nature
Suspension

Jenny Cloke Children
Oh!

Ellen Gamer Travel
Autumn In The Big Apple

Patricia Whitt Nature
Dawning Of A New Day

Pam Thomas Nature
Bird Of Paradise

Wendy Fobare Davis — Nature
Nature's Beauty

Ann Bateman — Children
Mud Madness

Casey Hurst — Portraiture
Love Of The Game

Lindsay Marie Seaburg — Animals/Pets
Dolphin Dream

Sze Sze Tobias — Nature
Punting In The Park

Freda Childress — Nature
Oh Deer, My Lunch!

Angelia Almazan   Nature
Lazy Afternoons

Arlene Durbin   Nature
Cloudy Silo

Beverly Moulton   People
Summer

Mary Ann Troester   Nature
Millennium Sunrise

Margie Young   Nature
Mother Nature's Beauty

Marjorie A. Mounts   Animals/Pets
Angel And Honey: Guardians Of The Light

Michael Phelan　　　　　　　　　　Children
Surfin' Son

Scott Quayle　　　　　　　　　　Nature
Morning's Light

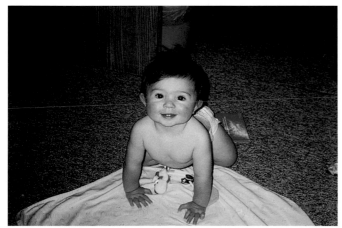

Donna Palkowski　　　　　　　　　Children
Twinkle, Twinkle, Little Star

Brian Kessler　　　　　　　　Animals/Pets
Cat In A Box

Sandra S. Brehm　　　　　　　　　Nature
God's Fireflies

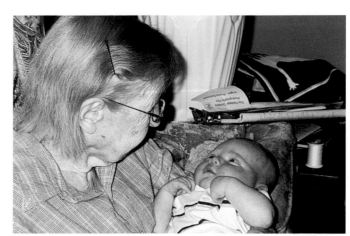

Esther Hesson　　　　　　　　　Children
First Meeting

Sherry Bradford Children
This Ford Is For You

Wanda M. Smith Nature
Red Sky In The Evening

Denice Hartigan Travel
Colosseum: Rome, Italy

Donald Conklin Nature
Fall Sunset

Ellen M. Dolan Other
Shady Characters

Milagros Estrada Travel
My Trip To St. John

Carole Small   Children
First Date

Ben Schein   Animals/Pets
The Duck

Arlene J. Rowles   Children
Hi, Grandma

Sarah Mullan   Nature
Meadow Pond

Gideon Dianon   Animals/Pets
I Am A Big Kitty

Lenard McCray   Nature
Picture Of Part Of Gensburg Markham Prairie

Wayland Horn Other
Gas Up To Fifty-Four Cents, What Will Be Next?

Pearl I. Queen Children
Hello Gran Dear, My Dear!

Rachel Brinklow Nature
Nature At Work

Terry Wood Humor
Wait For Me

Kimberly Rintz Nature
Jubilance

Sue Bohlmann Children
Dusk On All Hallows' Eve

Frances Williams Animals/Pets
Is This A Face Of A Devil?

Kourtni Reynolds Nature
God's Glory Shines

Amanda Murff Nature
Small Bits Of Heaven

Anna Carey Children
But We're In Love

Marilyn Shafron Nature
Owl Butterflies On Fruit

Linda Mearns Nature
Island Hideaway

Harold E. Smith Jr.   Nature
Sunset On Lake

Lorah Lynne Weesner   Nature
Lovely

Kathleen Broderick   Animals/Pets
Watchful Eye

Cheryl Nowatkowski   Animals/Pets
Red, White, And Blue Raccoon

Benjamin Summers   People
Old Teacher, Youngest Learner

Everett E. Dixon   Other
Two Children And Their Pet, Balivor

Michael L. Hardy Nature
End Of Day

Art Schrot Nature
Rainbow Falls

Anita Williams Nature
Moods Of Nature

Lisa A. Grady Animals/Pets
Emma's Day Out

Robert L. Bruner Travel
Twilight On Ottawa Beach

Elda L. Hollis Nature
Solitary

Patty Simpson   Animals/Pets
Honeycomb Cowfish

Tanya Danielle Day   Other
A Look Back

Ray Horneman   People
Renaissance Day

Carol Vega   Nature
Fuschia Feast

Jess Ellars   Nature
Untitled

Jennifer L. Lee   Children
Discovery

Karen Phelps   Animals/Pets
Baby And The Beast

Mae McHugh   Other
Time-Out

Patricia R. Tullis   Nature
Nature Beauty

Frank Kozlowicz   Nature
Mother On Guard

Margaret R. Roberts   Nature
Blue Velvet

Rachel Andrews   Nature
October Essence

Stefanie Johnson   Other
Untitled

Kenneth Terrell Collins   Other
Peace And Security

Wm. F. Ledford Sr.   People
After 9/11

Mathieu Pouliot   Other
Bird Of Steel

Tim Reuter   Nature
Heartland Sunset

Kristina Clark   Nature
Blooming Beauty

Jose L. Moreno   Travel
Mexotic Land

Melba Pannone   Travel
Highway Hazard

Brandon Cline   Other
The End

Jean F. Kimball   Nature
Mistycal Morning

Shannon Patrick   Children
It's Cold

Dessica DeVore   Travel
Ride To Alcatraz

Allison Raketti   Children
Overcoming Obstacles

Dilip Gandhi   Nature
Do You Feel The Heat?

Rosalie Blackman   Nature
New Mexico Sunset

Brooke Lee   Animals/Pets
Just A Taste

Barry L. Woody   People
Sisters: Ari And Sha-Sha

Ray L. House   Children
Children And Redwood

Cathy Heffner   People
Silent Wisdom

Kelly MacAusland   Children
Destination: Everywhere

Evelyn A. Young   Nature
Coming Of The Light

Helen Jane Schroeder   Nature
Pretty In Pink

Donna Pine   Other
This Old House

Tina M. Dillon   Children
Wonderment

Sybil Dodson-Lucas　　　　　　Nature
Dunes At Caprtee State Park

Leah Mabry　　　　　　Nature
Sunflowers In The Badlands

Jerry Sauer　　　　　　Nature
Forest Fire?

Lindsay Gayhart　　　　　　Nature
Memories

Diana Sinn　　　　　　Animals/Pets
Feeding The Ducks

Penny Lynn Jefferson　　　　　　Children
Life Outside The X-Box

Mary Lou Erelyn Spence Nature
Untitled

Linda McGrew Nature
After The Rain

Erin Morris Children
A Quiet Moment

Laura M. Matera Nature
Sunset At Grand Canyon

David Underwood People
The Men That Made Our Country

Darlene James Nature
Butterfly Rapture

Sharon Neely Children
In Deep Thought

Crystal Kuznik Animals/Pets
Birdie

Jane L. Waggoner People
Fun In The Sun

Carolina Castro Humor
Passion For Life

Lori Whitaker Action
Wiping Out With Style

Linda McFadden Animals/Pets
My Name Is Elvis, And I Ain't Nothing But A Hound Dog!

Alyce Barlowski   Animals/Pets
Reading Is Fun!

Darleen Strong   Animals/Pets
Life's A Beach

Yvette Metzger   Children
Named Innocence

Judith K. Dickinson   Nature
Warm Memories

Cathy Johnson   Nature
Indian Summer

Randi Patterson   People
For Pete's Sake

Maria Sherry People
Sunset From "A" Mountain

Danielle Erickson Humor
Finger Food?

Orra A. Mitchell Nature
Sunset In Massena, New York

Marilyn J. Eberle Children
Sister Talking After School

Richard Danell Nature
Tranquility

Carrie Wells-Young People
Sunday Sister

Lee Young Nature
Sky Of Fire

Edith Adlam Animals/Pets
Angels Watching Over

Patricia M. Powell Nature
Simple Beauty

Tara L. Furrh Children
Missin' Papa

April Clouse Humor
Just Chillin'

Dori Brandt Animals/Pets
Ah, The Sweetness Of A Texan Wildflower!

Natasha Batt Children
Clayton

Lyle Nielsen Nature
Winter Sunrise On Sand Lake

Donna M. Stone Animals/Pets
Lab Sleeping (It's All Mine)

Jeanie Paddock-Zimmerman Nature
Prairie Rose

Mabel Schroder Travel
Beautiful Sunset

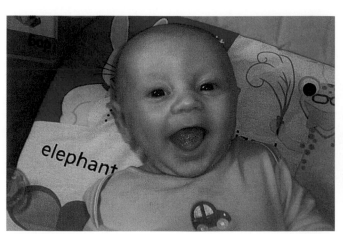

Dawn Firsing-Paris Children
Baby Shane

Glenn Ver Wey   Children
When Life Was Simple

Anthony Vignier   Animals/Pets
Fred At The Window

Maira Gutierrez   Nature
Mass Of Vapor, In The Sky

Jessica Caracciolo   Other
Home

Kathy Lake   Animals/Pets
Cloudy Skies In Cali/Colorado

Jonathan Silas   People
Hearts And Souls

Anna Hatten Children
Jon David

Louis Grady Children
White Serenity

Karen Chidester Children
A Boy's Quandary

Susan J. Lopatin Nature
Breaking The Water Barrier

Sister Beth A. Herrmann, O.S.F. Travel
Golden Temple, Kyoto, Japan

Karen Apker Nature
Majesty Revealed

Sherry Heier　　　　　　　　　　Humor
Parking Rules

Char Manning　　　　　　　　　　Nature
Summer Daze Gone By

Laura Mears　　　　　　　　　　Animals/Pets
Sandy Summer With Duke

Art Scherl　　　　　　　　　　Animals/Pets
All Things New

Helena Gijsbers Van Wijk　　　　　　　　　　People
The Land Of The Free, The Home Of The Brave

Sara Chalupnicki　　　　　　　　　　Animals/Pets
Pepper, The Cool Dog!

Lorene Garland   Nature
Crystal Morning

Cyndi Dague   Travel
Dominican Dreams

Linda Martinez   People
Hands Of A Generation

James Matthew Daneker   Children
What Matters Most

Rachel Bennett   Nature
R-R-Relaxing

Charles R. Beard Jr.   Animals/Pets
A Dog's Point Of View

Ruth Petrauskas   Animals/Pets
Champion

Gigi S. Skinner   Nature
Castle Mountain

Elyssa Quesada   People
Daydreamer

Ivette Ocejo   Children
Innocence

Keeli Rue   Children
Happiness Is . . .

Chureerat Shariffskul   Animals/Pets
My Cooling Spot

Thelma K. Miller   Other
Cleaning The Crib

Marion T. Cochrum   Nature
Attacking Owl

Pamela McVey   Other
Summertime

Ricky Malone   Nature
Lake Marie's Splendor

Rhyan C. Lange   Nature
Magical Power Of Water

Robbie Lambert   Portraiture
Miss Posey

Lucy Malack Children
Fishing On The Battenkill, Manchester, VT

Benjamin Knepp Other
Reach For The Sky, Reach For Your Dreams

Kathy Stevenson Nature
A Day In A Bug's Life

David D. Belding Nature
Spring Bloom

James Kelly Other
Wahsutat'ati

Larry Atkinson Children
Sunday Afternoon

Eric Droze Other
Abandoned

Deborah Lynn Starr Nature
Sunset On The Ohio

David A. Phillips II Other
Margie's Angel

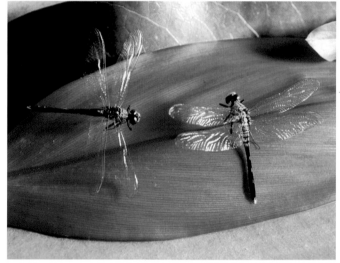

Al Di Martino Nature
Dragonflies

Emily Flom Sports
The Agony Of Defeat

Elaine Newlan Other
Serenity

Elly Michael   Nature
Spring In Bloom

Shannon Stump   Animals/Pets
Do You See What I See?

Patsy Wagoner   Other
Pot Of Gold From Heaven

Joan Pinsker   Children
Dazzled

Lori Carroll   Other
Railroad Roundhouse

Lacey Fitzgerald   Children
Leave Me Alone

Margaret A. Laakkonen   Nature
Monument Valley, Arizona

Mellonie Rucker   Animals/Pets
I'll Be Good

David B. Berson   Nature
Lily Pads

Sabrina Ximerez   Travel
Inspiration Speaks Out

Nicolette J. Wears   Nature
Mushroom Splendor

Dennell Guyette   Portraiture
Sun Ray Sister

Robert Schurter   Nature
How Many Hummingbirds In Picture?

Jason Duggan   Other
Untitled

Catherine L. Turner   Nature
Serenity

Tom White   Nature
Life In The Desert

Johnny Kinder   Nature
Texas Spring

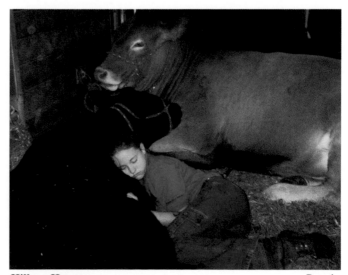

Hillary Henson   People
Trust And Love

Patricia Bata   Nature
Relentless Winter

Debbie L. Walter   Nature
Country Morning

Laurie Howard   Travel
Montana Rainbows

John DeBeau   Nature
Butterfly's First Flight

Louis Stout   Nature
The Beauty Of Nature At Jackson Hole

Judith Karen Beachler   Nature
I Think I'm In Bee Heaven

Sharrie Conly Children
Brooke

Charles P. Clark Animals/Pets
Love The Water

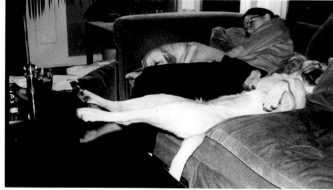

Sylvia J. Bowen Animals/Pets
Not Sleeping, Checkin' My Eyelids For Holes

Boris Golubov Nature
Glacier National Park

Linda Randall People
Father And Son

Margaret Ulatouski Animals/Pets
A Frog's Life

Bill Palfi   Nature
Magnificent Phantom

Patti Ardoin   Nature
The Egret Family

Nanci Le Van Valkenburg   Other
Peony Light Magic

Wes Harvey   People
Marissa Nicole

Bob Portsmouth   Nature
Evening Shades

Jaime Dobson   Nature
Eternal Sky

John Stephens   Other
Alaskan Sunset

Mimi Griffin Dudley   Nature
A Day Full Of Color

Vince Ward   Animals/Pets
Canada

Jacqueline Horn   Nature
Summer's Sweet Rewards

Roxy Olson   Nature
Country Fireworks

Kristi Ottosen   Action
The Burn

Kenneisha Walker Children
Christian

Annie Serra Nature
Tuolomne River, Yosemite High Country

Wanda Powell Nature
Let's Check The Birdhouse!

Alicia Zeien Nature
Reflections

Alex Wasilewski Animals/Pets
Keeping Watch

J. Kloepfer Travel
Red Rock Canyon, Waterton National Park, Canada

Ginger Bruce
Durnstein, Austria

Travel

Annette Turnbow
American River Dream

Nature

Trena Pratt
The Hay Field

Children

Camille Carideo
House Arrest

Humor

Suzanne Sanyoto
Rodeo Dreams

Children

Norma Wittmayer
A Precious Remnant Of Montana Diggins

Other

Crystal Lowers   Children
Little Angel?

Betty Baker   Nature
Yellowstone Sky Fire

Mitchell Arthur Wiley   Humor
A Man In A Dress

Roberta W. Hillman   People
Just Married

Manuel Pascual   Humor
Cloning A Bagpiper

Melissa Wheeler   Children
Could Use A Little Rain

Jennifer Picklesimer   Children
Sleepy Travelers

Kayla Carey   Nature
Silver Falls

R. Christopher Naughton   Nature
Pompous Parrots

Holly Browne-Mester   Other
Campus Constellation

Patricia Coats   Nature
Autumn Splendor

Ty Smith   Travel
Glowing Spires

Tasha L. Beckett   Nature
Honeymoon

John Wilzbacher   Nature
A Superstitious Awakening

Colleen V. Lancaster   Nature
A Cow's Skull

La Vonna John   Children
Poor Fishy

Rebecca Hirschman   Nature
Waters Of Fall

Carolyn D. McLean   Travel
Morning At Owls Head, Maine

Eileen Miller Children
Natural Beauty

Katrina Pearl Children
Daniel

Burlyn V. Hanson Nature
Flowers Of Summer

Bernie Bisbee Travel
Interstate 15: Utah

Austin Anderson Nature
Weird Deer

Darla Hollingshead People
Veteran Reflection

Tom Anderson   Nature
A Million Years Of Hard Work

Jason Hann   Nature
A Day In The Sun

Steve Dale   Travel
Poulsbro Shadows

Michael E. Bates   Nature
Fire In The Sky

Andrew E. Stevens   Animals/Pets
The Feast

Nora Naylor   Other
The Young And The Old

Shanna Comstock   Other
The Game Of Life

Rebecca L. Peterson   Animals/Pets
Why Is The Baby Crying?

Christen Rhodes   Nature
Niagra Falls At Night

Corrie Graves   Nature
Morning Glory

Susan James   Travel
On The Road Through Pebble Beach

Jessica Hall   Nature
A Good Night Kiss From Above

Lark Bearden   Nature
Untitled

Michael Martin   Other
Springtime, Youngs Vineyard, Shenandoah Valley, CA

Frances E. Tourdot   Nature
Storm's Comin'

Lisa Cannizzaro   Nature
Shadows On The Beach

Ashley Brown   Sports
Ol' Glory

Eliot Aust   Nature
A Migrating Bird's Plea

Amber Whipp　　　　　　　　Nature
Androsian Sunrise

Tom Mollison　　　　　　　　Nature
Alpine Fir At Spray Falls

Jarred Hendrix　　　　　　　　Nature
Sunflower Dreams

Kristopher W. Kimmel　　　　　　Nature
Androsian Sunset

Matthew Conner　　　　　　　Nature
Gorilla Stare

Rich Marquez　　　　　　　Nature
Sunrise At Sunrise Shores

Maggie Crabtree   Nature
Mountain Stream

Gwendolyn Chrest   Travel
A Slice Of Liberty

Sarah Williams   Other
Windmill Mailbox

Toni Linde   Travel
Bodie, NV

Suzanne Newman Terlitz   Nature
Courtship In Flight

Laurie Schwan   People
Pondering The Future

Ann Degnan   Children
My Prince?

Hannelore Hanks   People
A Girl's Best Friends

Kim Adams   Animals/Pets
Playing In The Flowers

Nathan Smith   Other
Sculpted Village

Erica Lee   Travel
Arbroath Chapel

Laura Paris-Sandler   Nature
Sunset On Cape May, New Jersey Beach

Jenni Lynne Colby   Nature
Devil's Gate

Elizabeth Irle   Nature
Angel Sun Dog

Tammie Smith   Travel
The Wrath Of the Euphrates

Brandon Ronald Spadoni   Nature
Who's Watching Who?

Richard L. White   People
Massai Herdsman Of Tanzania

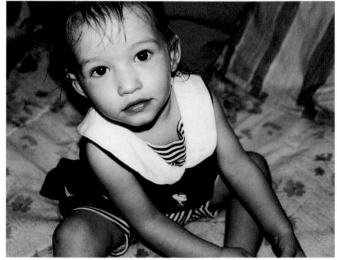

Ariel Simpson   Children
Alexia

Edward Shortridge   Nature
Misty Maine Morning

Didzis Bremze   Nature
Nu Kas I Ko!

Anastasia Lucignani   Nature
Boardwalk

Em Rojas   Travel
Louisville Meter Watcher

Pat Bilby Teeters   Nature
Big Sky Country

Lynn Stalnaker   Portraiture
Self-Portrait: View From The Cheap Seats

Wanda Angel   Animals/Pets
Sasha

Alla Selivanova   Nature
Nightfall And City

Maria Straka   Animals/Pets
Horses Stroll

Yoshiko Rhodes   Children
Curious Children

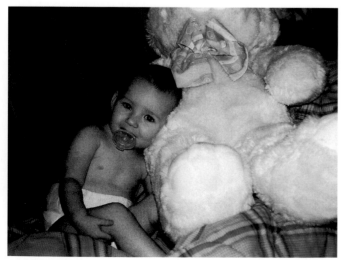

Vickie A. Hall   Children
Precious Baby And Her Bunny Bear

Jimmy Chen   Portraiture
Principal Cellist

Hattie Dawn Prenger   Nature
God's Glorious Creation

Barbara R. Krasner   Nature
Arbor In Chanticleer

Andrew Margolin   Other
Fountain In Charleston

Cristina Dufek   Nature
Grandpa's Pond

Paul Gilson   Animals/Pets
Loving Swims On The Avon River

Edward Richard Sanders   Nature
At The Pond

Rodney H. Travis — Nature
Valley Fog

Gordon L. Speirs — People
Rickshaw On Miyajima Island, Japan

Robert Tamburello — People
Greek Man Waiting At Taxi Stand

Lori Caruthers — Nature
Just Passing Through

John Travis Bradford — Other
The Other Side

Tracey Pinto — Travel
Green Peace

Christina Gothie   Children
Simple Love

Heather Broughton   Children
Fun In The Sun

Alison K. Riordan   Animals/Pets
Swan

Mavis Eldridge   Children
Did I Miss The Party?

Kristan E. Hafeman   Nature
A View From A Face

Crystal Valdez   Children
Guten Tag From Germany

Navonna Browning   Children
Can't Catch Me!

Jack L. Mooney   Children
See My Band-Aid, Papa!

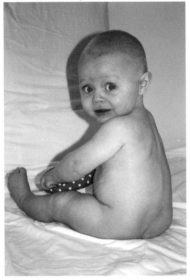

Nicole Lindell   Children
Bambino

Terry Legge   Other
Crystal

ARTISTS'
PROFILES

ADAMS, KIM R.
This picture of my youngest daughter, Emery, was taken in the late afternoon on her eighth birthday on June 26, 1998. She was adorned with a birthday crown that she had punched out of a birthday card that had just arrived in the mail from her paternal grandmother. This is a priceless family photo of our "Queen Of The Jungle," a title so fitting of a little girl who was always so dazzled by nature. This photo was captured as she climbed a fig tree outside our home in LaGrange, Georgia while waiting for her birthday entourage of friends to arrive for her party.

ALMAZAN, ANGELIA
This photo was taken while on vacation in Mexico. I was having lunch with friends and I saw this rare, beautiful sight approaching the restaurant. So I took a moment for I would not forget.

AN, YOUNGSOOK
This picture was taken when my baby was nine-and-a-half months old. I heard from many friends he looks like a boy and can go to school with a big backpack. He was always serious when he got pictures taken, and it was really hard for me to catch his smiling face. It was at the mall in Minnesota where I spent my first winter vacation with my baby and husband. When my husband went to work, I brought my baby to the mall near my house. He loved to spend time at play and he was the youngest baby there. Now he has started to dance and all my family members are happy for him. He is the most precious thing in my life and my husband and I wish to have his sister in the future.

ANDERSON, MARK P.
Late May is a beautiful time in Wisconsin. It's warm, lush, abundant, and full of life and regrowth. The whitetail fawn in the photograph was as inquisitive as I was during a walk on our farm on that warm spring morning. The tension finally became too great for the young deer, and when he ventured out of the gooseberry bushes to get a better view of the intruder, I took the picture. My wife, Bonnie, and my children, Nicholas and Natalie, often see deer, turkeys and other wildlife on our farm, located in southwestern Wisconsin.

ANDRADE, SILVIA BEATRIZ
When I traveled to Pisac, Peru, I fell in love with Catalina's smile, this little girl that is just waiting for a lot of people around her, looking. What is she thinking? Most importantly, what is she feeling? I couldn't let this priceless, magic moment pass. I'm working in a research center taking scientific photographs in the electronic microscopy, but the most important thing to me is discovering every moment of life, asking how? With my camera, I can catch each moment while traveling and enjoying the peoples, cultures, and places of the world.

ANGEL, WANDA
This is a photo of a kitten we rescued from the local animal shelter. We got her for my granddaughter, Alyssa. The picture was totally not posed. We had had Sasha for about two weeks when this picture was taken. Sasha had disappeared for a while and we were looking for her. I just happened to look down into a cardboard box

Alyssa had been playing with. There in the box were several of Alyssa's small stuffed animals and Sasha. She seemed to be saying: "They will never find me here." I hurried for my camera to get this picture, as I could not have posed a better one in a million years.

ANTONIO, CAROL L.
We have a two-person jacuzzi tub that our girls, Lily and Samantha, love to take a bath in. John had daddy duty while I was out shopping. When I got back home, the tub was literally overflowing with bubbles. They had put only a capful in the water but they turned on the jets and almost instantly the tub was fluffy white. The girls had so much fun decorating themselves and each other. It took about forty-five minutes to make all the bubbles to dissipate. We won't be doing that too many more times, although it did take away the winter blahs for a while.

ARAND, JASON
I am originally from Union, MO, now living in St. Louis with my wife, Angela, and son, Kyan. My subjects in this photo are my nephew, Aaron, who was five years old at the time, and our pet tree frog, Cutie, whom Aaron proudly named. I love photos like this one when I catch people with natural reactions as if the camera isn't there.

ARHIN, TAMARA RENEE
This is our son, Landon Ekow Arhin, at one month old. I've always liked the black and white contrast and imagined this shot in my head before he was born. I believe that it turned out even better than I imagined. I take pictures of my family all of the time, but I am not a photographer. I do imagine creative ideas from time to time.

ARMSTRONG, REGINA
This photo was taken from my deck, overlooking the ocean off the coast of Maine, where I witness many beautiful sunrises, sunsets, summer rainbows, northeaster's storms, fog rolling in off the ocean, and eerie winter sea smoke. The scenery is forever changing. To live here is a nature lover's paradise. I call it my little corner of heaven.

AWAD, DAWN L.
This photo was taken in Central Park. My new camera and the trip to NYC were gifts from my husband for my fortieth birthday. This is a week I will never forget!

BAER, OLGA
The elements of surprise and adventure are what draw me to photography. To catch the ephemeral moment, stop time with a click of the shutter, and thus capture an activity or a fleeting expression is a highly rewarding experience. In this photograph, I have caught my cat, Tiger, in a relaxed and contemplative moment. What is he thinking about?

BARES, BETHANY
Winter greetings from Bethany Bares, four-month-old daughter of Donna and John Bares. This photo was taken at Riverview Camp for girls in Mentone, AL, where I am the Assistant Director. As our youngest camper, Bethany loves all the attention she receives. Since Mentone is on top of Lookout Mountain, we do enjoy snow in

the winter months! She was dressed for winter weather when we took this photo.

BARNES, ROBERT D., SR.
Success comes from taking advantage of every opportunity that is presented in everything, not just photography. I almost missed this shot. I had to go get the camera and when I returned, they had separated. I waited and they resumed their fight. I remember missing shots which I could enjoy now, if only I had taken the time to capture them. Next week, tomorrow, or an hour later, is too late, nothing is the same.

BATA, PATRICIA
I live on a farm and assist my husband and son in growing wheat and barley crops. This untimely sleet storm occurred May 11-13, 2004, seriously delaying our seeding, thus a frost damaged our crops in the fall. I am learning digital photography and computer functions and love the challenge. I am sixty-five years old and I am a pianist, church organist, mother of five, and grandmother of eight. I grow a huge garden, operate a combine and truck during harvest season and ride a Honda motorcycle on the prairie trails of northeastern North Dakota with my grandson.

BATES, MICHAEL E.
It is indeed an honor and joy to have my photo recognized and published in this publication. It's a pleasure to show the beauty that's all around us. "Fire In The Sky" is just one example of the creator's masterpiece. It's my hope that we as people can see the beauty in each other. I hope this picture will bring joy to all that view it.

BAY, REGINA
The "American Dream" title came from the three decades of hard work that I put towards my gardening, flower arrangements, and photography. The Nandima berries and Persimmon symbolize a gesture of obtaining successful results. The dragon eye pine is a symbol of longevity. The Ama lilies along with pine centered in the vase act as a focal point. The light gray vase stands out superbly with red flowers and berries. This is ideal for a winter flower arrangement with use of colorful materials. The flowers make surroundings bright and cheerful in the beginning of the year.

BEACHLER, JUDITH KAREN
People do not realize the beauty around us and the importance of nature and its creatures. There are many things we can learn by watching around us. These creatures large and small are all valuable to our existence, such as a tiny bee shown in this photo. I prefer to photograph nature and animals because they show many beautiful things surrounding us that we rarely see.

BECKER, DEB
It was a morning of peaceful, frosted splendor and I was going to enjoy it. I set out with my camera to attempt to capture some of the splendor. My friends, Abu, Chip, T Bone, and Lucky, were curious, yet they peacefully waited as I finished clicking off ten rolls of film. I am blessed that my picture will be published so I can share with you a piece of that peaceful, trusted splendor.

BECKETT, TASHA L.
This photo was taken on my wonderful honeymoon in Cancun, Mexico. It shows the beauty of a relaxing time in a hammock between two beautiful palm trees while watching the waves crashing into the pier. I am blessed with a wonderful husband, Jesse, and a beautiful daughter, Krislyn. I am a beauty consultant with Mary Kay Cosmetics and my dream is to be a wedding and landscaping photographer.

BEH, MING MING
This is a photo of myself. I wore a silver gown dress with a mask for a ball (prom). My hair was dyed and curled up. My own hands made this mask. When I arrived at the ball, everyone suddenly turned to see me. Everyone was unable to stop telling me how amazing and gorgeous I looked in the gown and mask, with my curled hair. I was selected to enter a competition for the best mask with others. When I got up on the stage, I received the biggest cheers from the audience I've ever had. I won the best mask and received a huge bottle of wine. I just felt so proud of this and really happy. I love this picture because it inspires me.

BERG, SARAH
This is a picture of my cat, "Tigger." I was trying to photograph her with my new camera and she just kept hiding. Here is the finished product. Enjoy!

BIDWELL, ROGER
I have always lived in Johnson and I enjoy taking pictures as a hobby. This picture is a plant in my wife's flower garden. I take pictures of her flowers to give her a photographic history to keep of the gardens she loves.

BIEDLER, GREGG ALLAN
Some pictures you see every day, some you don't. On this day while walking through the local zoo, we found the gorillas frolicking in the snow. The zookeepers told us that this was the first time they experienced snow. They were very much intrigued by it. I've been taking pictures most of my life and I enjoy it immensely. My wife, Kristi, and I have decided to take it one step further by submitting this photograph to see where it takes us.

BINKOWITZ, CHARLES
I was born on April 13, 1952 in Brooklyn, NY. My parents are Harvey and Marilyn. I married Connie on February 14, 1995, with whom I have three children, Danielle, Steven, and Aaron. I attended Memphis College of Art. I work in Sales Outside. I was a Finalist in the Best of College Photography 1996. My photos were sent to President Clinton and Congress to help amend the Amerasian reform bill. I had photographs published in River City Contemporary and The First Supper. What I enjoy most is photographing new refugee families.

BISBEE, BERNIE
This picture was taken on a trip that I took with my sister in the fall of 2003. I traveled from South Dakota to Colorado to meet up with her. We then traveled to New Mexico and California to visit other family members. On our way back, we had to stop in Vegas to try our luck. We traveled through Utah, where I took the picture. Finally,

we made our way back to Colorado, then the final stretch for me was traveling alone back to Aberdeen, South Dakota. On the trip, while my sister was doing most of the driving, I sat in the passenger's seat and took a lot of scenic pictures. I kept the camera handy so I could take a picture at a moment's notice. It was great fun!

BLACKFORD, MIKKI
For as long as I can remember, I have always wanted to be an artist. I never imagined that I would have such a great passion until I got a camera in my hand. People say that I have a unique way of seeing the world and its natural wonders. I love to manipulate objects to a different point of view, as seen in my waterfall image. Art is all about being different and creating new and interesting ways to see an object or point of view and I love the fact that the possibilities are endless.

BLAKE, JENNIFER
This is a picture I took for a 4-H photography project. It is a photo of my cousin, Mason, riding a John Deere pedal tractor in our field. The tractor belonged to my grandfather when he was growing up. My family has been involved with agriculture for over 100 years. This photo holds a special meaning for our family in hopes that future generations will continue the legacy.

BOERO, LUCA
The eyes of mountain gorillas are something hard to forget. An exhausting trek within the Ugandan/Rwandan or DRC slippery mountains is worth the magical encounters with these relatives. Their facial expressions are something that won't be forgotten. This photo gives just a little example. I hope that this image will give the readers of this book an idea of the feelings that arise in meeting these creatures, one of the most endangered species on Earth. Only 700 of them, more or less, are still alive.

BOHLMANN, SUE
This photo is of my daughters, Allison and Jessica, on a perfect night. As we all know, kids grow up way too fast. I love to take pictures of them as often as I can. My husband, Troy, and I also have a son named Toby. We live on a small farmette with dogs, cats, ducks, chickens, and pigs. We enjoy the outdoors and camping.

BOROVY, DENNIS
This is a great honor. I always believed my picture taking was good, but being selected as one of the best is incredible. My three boys and I love to vacation in Maine and I love to take pictures of our trips. Maine is truly a vacation land and postcard picture-perfect. I am looking forward to seeing the book and my plaque when they arrive. They will always have a special spot in my home.

BORRAS, ROY
This photograph is of my seventy-five-year-old father and ten-month-old daughter, taken on Father's Day. I wanted to demonstrate contrast in different ways: black and white, male and female, young and old, hence the title, "Generation." Photography has been a hobby of mine for many years. Over the last five years or so, I've been taking it more seriously. I've been educating myself

by reading photography books and magazines, analyzing the style of various photographs and enrolling in a variety of courses. Working full-time and raising a family keeps me pretty busy, but I always make time for my passion, photography.

BOWEN, SYLVIA J.
My name is Proud Winter Moon. However one looks at me though, I should have been a tiger. It's just good that I live with someone who owns (and uses) her camera. Sometimes I pose but other times (like this one) she can be a real sneak. She owns a SLR 35mm camera and has her eye on a Canon Digital SLR, heaven forbid!

BOYER, TED
Here are the three daughters of Mark and Lora Seymour of Hershey, PA. Emily, age six, is checking for the mail, Darby, age two, is checking for the merchandise, and Shey, age five, is checking to see if Pop Pop, the cameraman, gets it right. Ted and Emily Boyer, of Souderton, PA, have nine grandchildren, and they take pictures every time they get a chance because their grandchildren are prettier and smarter than all other grandchildren.

BREHM, SANDRA S.
I am a sixty-two-year-old great-grandmother that enjoys God's sunset creations. I took a lot of pictures, but sunrises and sunsets are my favorite. I have taken sunsets from Ohio to Oregon. I thank God for the privilege of viewing his wonderful creations.

BREMZE, DIDZIS
This picture is taken during my exchange year in Switzerland. It is on the Alps, on the Mountain Nouneol, Melchisee Frutt. It's about 3,000 meters above the sea level and it's so warm that you can sit in your underwear and won't be cold. I love the mountains and try to spend my free time in them, by snowboarding for the past eight years. A special thanks goes to Lauri Lepik.

BRIGGS, KEITH
Driven by the love of my life, my daughter, Ailantra, this photo simply portrays the purity and innocence of youth. I tried to capture the natural hunger to learn that children display. This photo also captures a moment in time for me.

BRINKLOW, RACHEL
A few years ago, I tried my hand at painting landscapes and this picture was taken with the intention to do a painting of it. The beauty of the colors captured in this photo was so spectacular. We knew it had to be shared. This picture of a mine's tailings pond was taken after the mine closure. It represents the end of one era and a new beginning of nature's reclamation.

BROCHU, SUZANNE G.
We were just driving around the back roads of Vermont. As we continued, my boyfriend, Hale, mentioned that this road was a cow path when he was younger. Now it was developed and we saw a house made of cobblestone. Hale, being a carpenter, was amazed, so we found this nature trail and found Sterling Falls Gorge, where at one time there was an old mill. All of a sudden, I turned around and saw this tree growing on a rock. I had

to rush home, get my camera, and take a picture of the Vermont tree determined to grow. The tree is still there to this day and growing. It is a Hemlock and eighteen inches in diameter.

BRODERICK, KATHLEEN
Our Jack Russell terrier, Butterfly, is the January pinup dog for the 2005 Jack Russell Calendar, published by Jasper Publications Inc. in Rhinebeck, NY. Instead of signing pawgraphs, Butterfly flits through our gardens, chasing squirrels and chipmunks. She eventually settles in the flowers to guard the hole in the base of the tree. On the other days, Butterfly brings gentle love and laughter to my mom and her friends at a senior living facility. She's the love of our life. It is a delightful challenge capturing her antics on film.

BRODIE, CHARLOTTE ANN
This special moment was captured when my best friend's husband was kissing his sweet Julia. She truly is an angel. I took this photo for all daddies everywhere who love their little girls.

BROUGHTON, HEATHER
This is a photo of my son, Abraham (a.k.a. The Ham), at his favorite place, the beach. As you can see, he's truly in his element in the sand and Lake Michigan not far off. My husband, Bill, and I love taking Abraham to the beach and nearby state park. My camera normally comes with us. I love to take pictures of Abraham and of nature itself; but when I can put Abraham and nature together, those are my favorite photos.

BROWN, CHRISTOPHER ROBERT
I am an amateur photographer who likes to carry my camera everywhere. My nature photo was taken in front of Taco Bell on a day with many storm clouds. I saw the sky and said to myself: "Look, a stairway to Heaven." At that moment, I took out my camera and click, the picture happened. I enjoy taking pictures and welcome the opportunity to be published here.

BROWNE-MESTER, HOLLY
This image was taken while I was a student at James Madison University in Harrisonburg, Virginia. The photograph was taken on campus at night using a star filter and 35mm camera. Inspiration for creating this image came from the works of Brassai. I enjoy the atmospheric and unknown quality that a high contrast picture creates. I live in beautiful Monroe County, West Virginia with my husband, Alex. I am an art teacher, preschool teacher and artist.

BROWNING, NAVONNA
This photo is of my daughter, Taylor Michelle, who was two-and-a-half years old at the time. It was taken at Chief Logan Park, where we live in West Virginia. Taylor was letting her true nature and spirit show as I took this photo. You can just see the fun and playfulness captured in her eyes. As a new photographer with my first experience with black and white, I couldn't be more pleased with the result, as I have a beautiful memory of my little girl at that age.

BUCK, VERA
I live where I work, which is to say it's an auto-

mobile salvage yard. To keep some kind of separation, I have planted several rose bushes around the house. Throughout the summer and fall, the bushes bloomed and were gorgeous with big, fragrant yellow roses. It was early one morning towards the end of the year while examining the bushes that this particular rose with dew on it was caught snapping away. Even as a child, with my first Brownie camera, I enjoyed taking pictures.

BURGESS, DOROTHY E.
This picture was taken in Fall River, Massachusetts the day after the blizzard of '05. It snowed all night and we had over two feet of snow. The combination of strong swirling winds and light powdery snow created these really beautiful designs.

CACHIA, JAYNE
This is my son, Jacob, at age two. His fascination with the light from a candle was wonderful to watch. Capturing it on film made it even more special.

CANNIZZARO, LISA
For as long as I can remember, I have always loved photography. The hundreds of pictures my mom has taken throughout my childhood inspired me to want to take pictures myself. In high school, I took photography classes where I learned to develop black and white photos. From that point on, I was hooked. My favorite pictures are close-ups. I like the idea of taking something ordinary and letting people see it differently. This is why I was drawn to this fence at Jones Beach. I am currently in college for elementary education and continue to take photography classes.

CARPENTER, WILLIAM
I took this photograph at the tulip farms north of Seattle. This outcast tulip was misplaced in a patch of red tulips. The black and white film helped create a more dramatic image. I used a burning and dodging technique in the darkroom to darken the corners and put more focus on the tulip. My hope is that my photographs will touch you or open your eyes to another point of view or another way of thinking. Soon I plan to attend film school and go on to create films as another way to express my views and creative talent.

CARR, MELINDA
This train engine is very unique in that it is one of the last functioning steam engines in America. It is from an era gone by, however, you can experience just a little bit of it when it makes one of its random stops across the country for visitors to come aboard. My husband, Roy, has worked for Union Pacific Railroad for twenty-five years. For fourteen of those years, he has been an engineer. He is very proud of his job and I am very proud of him. "The Challenger" came through our hometown last summer and made a short stop for visitors. I could not resist. My grandson, Christian, and I had to go for a souvenir and a photo.

CARROLL, LORI
Capturing both the past and the present has always been a passion of mine. Patiently waiting for the exact moment to capture that perfect image has become very important to me. On a trip to

Greenfield Village in Dearborn, MI, capturing the past was easy; finding the exact moment to open the shutter was the challenge. On this day, my patience was rewarded.

CARTER, NANCY L.
I took this picture one morning while I was getting ready for work. Baron is seven months old in this picture and so very smart! He likes sitting on the edge of the bed so I have his complete attention. Luckily, he stayed put while I grabbed the camera, so I could capture that adorable face. I have taken quite a few pictures of him, but I thought this picture turned out better than the rest! It was easy though, because Baron is such a ham and quite photogenic!

CASPER, JUDY A.
Adventure beyond my wildest dreams was found while kayaking the Rock Islands of Palau in the far Pacific. Multi-colored coral, giant clams, caves and exotic fish were sighted during the six-hour kayaking journey of the island. Bound by the Pacific Ocean to the east and the Philippine Sea to the west, I was captured by the endless beauty of the scenic treasures that will last a lifetime through my photography.

CAUDILL, ANITA A.
This is in loving memory of our grandson, Brian Ray Crawford. On February 1, 2004, at the age of twenty-four, our grandson was killed in a vehicle accident. The picture is of our youngest daughter, Karen Sue and Brian's daughter, our great-granddaughter, Calli, who was turning two on February 12, 2004. This picture was taken the day after the funeral as the family gathered to discuss the accident and remember the life of a father, son, brother, grandson, nephew, cousin, and friend.

CHALUPNICKI, SARA
I am a huge animal lover and I love to take pictures. My dog has been with me most of my life. I wanted to see if I could get some pictures of him. He posed for every picture as if he was meant to be in front of the camera. His name is Pepper and he is a cocker spaniel.

CHANCE, BOB
"The whole Earth is full of his glory," Isaiah 6:3. Nowhere is this more evident to me than in nature. Flowers are the most beautiful, most delicate, and most intricate of all. In them, I see the infinite knowledge and wisdom of our Creator as well as His immense love for us, His children. Why else would He fill the whole Earth with the kind of beauty and splendor as the flower in this picture except for our enjoyment? Indeed, the whole Earth is full of His glory. Alleluia.

CHANG, KAO XU
Who could resist this precious face? I played hooky from work to visit my nephews and niece in California. We had never been to Sea World and look at what we found! Miss you guys! Love always, your auntie Kaoxu.

CLARK, CHARLES P.
As my family and I sat down for dinner at an oceanfront restaurant in Hawaii, I spotted a dog and his master on the beach playing with a

Frisbee. The man on the beach began throwing the Frisbee into the ocean and every time, the dog would retrieve the Frisbee after spending a few minutes swimming around looking for it. The dog became an audience pleaser and seemed to enjoy entertaining all of us with a camera.

CLARKE, JOSEPH PHILIP

This photo is of my dog called Ninoy. Just before Christmas '04, I bought my first digital camera. I started to take a couple photos of him, but I found it was so hard to keep him still and he would sniff the camera. Then one night, I got my camera out to take photos of the Christmas tree and I saw him just sitting there. I turned around and I finally got the photo you see. My parents, Merlyn and Trevor, couldn't believe how I got such a good photo of him. I will cherish this photo forever.

CLIFT, HEATHYR

I took this photograph of my father in 1999 when I was just beginning to explore photography. He was a great sport, posing for me in many photographic experiments, including this one. I never imagined it would turn out to be so amazing. It is still, and will always be one of my favorites. The photo has a dreamy, mystical quality to it that I love. In it, my father seems to have been transformed into a wizard intently focused on his magical task of "Harnessing The Light." I feel that not only conveys a sense of wonder, but more importantly, it honors the special bond that I have with my father, who holds the key to who I am and who I shall become.

CLINE, BRANDON

This photograph was taken on one of my outdoor adventures on the farm. History has always been one of my interests, and the old posts caught my eye. I could only imagine what they had seen and felt during their lifetime, the seasons they endured and the people and animals that they had been witness to. I felt the need to capture them and be witness to them. This is my favorite photograph that I have taken, and I felt that it should be shared.

CLOUSE, APRIL

I love to take pictures. I am known as the picture lady. If anyone needs a picture of something, more than likely I have it. They are my memories. We all make friends in our lives; they come and go. What better way to keep them close to your heart, than a picture?

COLBY, JENNI LYNNE

I am a tenth grade student at Enterprise High School in Utah. I took this picture in Wyoming while on family vacation in the summer of 2002. We had followed the pioneer trail westward from Navoo, IL past such landmarks as Chimney Rock and Independence Rock. This picture is a favorite reminder of my family's journey to rediscover our pioneer heritage. This scene at Devil's Gate is one my ancestors probably enjoyed as they made their journey over 150 years ago.

COLLINS, KENNETH TERRELL

I live in a large major city known for its buildings, traffic and danger. Here I have found a spot in the city that seems miles and miles away and is peaceful and secure.

COLLINS, LORA

This is the sight that most people get when they walk into my home. It has become one of the most popular conversation subjects. Spaz was my thirty-fifth birthday present from my husband, and the best one I ever got.

COMSTOCK, SHANNA

I grew up in an artistic family and I have always envied my mother's abilities. I have explored many art forms and expressions. I started taking pictures at a young age, but it wasn't until I took a high school photography class that I really got serious. This photograph was created from a light and shadow assignment given by my teacher, Ms. Csavina. The world needs more teachers like her. Her passion, humor, and inspiration have truly influenced my photography and me. If it weren't for her and my mother, I wouldn't be where I am today.

CONNOLLY, ROBERTA

This photograph was taken while I was home in Maine for a weekend. I moved to New Hampshire nine years ago. I spend time at least once a month with family and friends in Maine. I love taking photos of the ocean, coastal towns, people, animals and nature. I now live on a lake that affords me the great opportunity of beautiful photography during all four seasons. I enjoy kayaking, biking, camping, hiking, cross-country skiing, and snowshoeing.

COOK, DENNIS G.

I love taking pictures, and I'm always ready to snap one. I'm looking for different images all the time. I take a lot of photos of nature, scenery, and animals. One of my shots won a contest in a local newspaper. It became part of a calendar. I don't take too many action shots, but I was pleased with the picture of RJ jumping into the pool.

COOK, GINA

When I look at my daughter's beautiful face, I realize this world can't be as bad as I sometimes think it is. This picture describes so many words to me, beauty, happiness, love, innocence, and peacefulness, "Without A Care In The World!"

COTTON, TAMI DOLEZAL

This photo was taken for Halloween 2001 when our daughter, Sterling Grace, was three months old. We carved a pumpkin and placed our angel in it. We only took a few pictures, as the pumpkin was cold and the tears began to flow shortly after we captured this priceless photo. Sterling Grace is the highlight of our lives and I have absolutely enjoyed capturing her every move on film to cherish forever.

COX, MISTY

Taking photos is something I have always enjoyed doing. Recently, with the help of friends and family, I have had the opportunity to express my love and enthusiasm for photography. This photo was captured during my first photo shoot. Morgen is the son of James and Stacey York. Morgen has these amazing blue eyes that convey the innocence of childhood. I was astonished at how well this photo turned out.

CRUMP, WAYNE

I love to take pictures of animals, especially birds. That's why my wife calls me Birdbrain. At least I think that's why. Anyway, I'm blessed to live on the Nature Coast of Florida, where I have many places to go and take pictures, this Tufted titmouse was in my front yard waiting on me.

DANELL, RICHARD

This picture was taken in the Montana Rocky Mountains near benchmark. Its title expresses the serenity of the subject matter and location. I hope others enjoy this peaceful scene as much as I do. Taking and sharing pictures has added joy to the senior portion of my life.

DARR, JAN

I have always enjoyed taking pictures when I travel and Arizona is one of my favorites for its natural beauty. This giant saguaro is on my sister-in-law Barbara's land and I took this picture because I was overcome with the huge size and number of years it took this giant cactus to grow. I wanted to share its beauty with my family back home in the east.

DAVENPORT, BETTY D.

This is Kimberly Holt, my first grandchild. She is about two years old. She liked the bucket to rinse her feet in better than she liked the pool. That's OK. We just loved having her with us.

DAVIS, JONATHAN

This is a photo of the U.S.S. Arizona Memorial I took while vacationing in Hawaii with my wife, Regina, my sister, Elizabeth, and her husband, William. While taking pictures, I noticed the way the American flag was waving and attempted to capture its symbolism. Being on the U.S.S. Arizona Memorial invoked deep emotion and sadness for the lives that were lost. I noticed the solemn looks on the faces of the men, tears that were being wiped by the women, and even the quiet of the children as though they, too, realized that they were standing on someone's grave. The Memorial itself is a beautiful architectural structure and I would recommend visitors touring Hawaii make the U.S.S. Arizona Memorial a must-see.

DAVIS, LISA L.

Taking pictures is one of my very favorite things to do. I love photographing my family, our pets and our vacations. I have oodles of photo albums that remind us of all the fun memories we've shared, how truly blessed we are, and how good God has always been in our lives. I'm so amazed he created such precious gifts as our son, Noah, and our Sunny D. Noah and I sing "You Are My Sunshine" to her often because she is an ever-present ray of light in our home. She's our sweet baby girl and is loved so much.

DAVIS, WENDY FOBARE

In the fast paced life we live, it is often easy to enjoy the pleasure of a beautiful, spring day without ever seeing the wonders of God's land. It is with the still frame of photography that God's amazing wonders are captured. "Nature's Beauty" is just one of those wonders.

DEBEAU, JOHN
My name is John DeBeau and I am eleven years old. I am attending Zenda Charter School in Zenda, Kansas. The students in our school were given handheld computers this year and encouraged to take pictures as well as learn how to do other things with them. Our superintendent's wife brought cocoons to our classrooms for us to watch as they developed into butterflies. The picture shows the butterfly from our room when we placed it outside for the first time. It sat on a leaf until it took off for its first flight.

DETTONE, DEBRA
It has always been a dream of mine to learn photography, but I always took too many pictures to be able to afford film developing. This particular year, I spent a great deal of money on a wonderful digital camera. I bought the camera around the sweetest day and since I always bought my mom flowers for the occasion, I wondered how I could afford them this year. I knew that I couldn't, so I went to her house, sat down on the floor, and began shooting pictures of her dog, Lacey. At first she didn't want to cooperate, but then she came over, dropped her ball in front of me and sat as if to pose for this picture. For the sweetest day, my mom received this picture and she said it was the best gift she ever received.

DEVORE, DESSICA
I was on a family weekend vacation in San Francisco and we decided to go to Alcatraz. This picture was taken from the boat on the way to Alcatraz. I am a student at Brooks Institute of Photography in Santa Barbara, California. I am learning that there is always a unique way to look at something ordinary, and there is always a great picture waiting to be taken, but you have to look for it and be ready when you see it.

DICKINSON, JUDITH K.
This picture captures the warm memories of a visit to my son, Scott, after many years apart. The meadows were full of wildflowers and sunshine as we drove on a dirt road over the mountains. It is a journey I will never forget.

DOBIAS, PAUL
Have I really been walking around with a camera for twenty-five years? This was taken at the Philadelphia Dragon Boat races. It was ninety-six degrees, and a concessionaire had just dumped out an ice chest. A malamute, a breed that really doesn't like heat, lumbered directly into the ice. Upon realizing he had four feet in ice, he lay down and refused to move.

DOBSON, JAIME
This photo was taken years ago on a warm May day. I was at the Willows in Salem, MA, where I lived most of my life, when I climbed down one of the rock walls. I had spent many days of my young childhood here near the ocean and find myself continually returning to this part of the shoreline with my camera. This is just one of many shots, but for some reason, this one continues to stand out. After years of shooting, this print still resonates and it would seem that others are attracted to it as well.

DODSON-LUCAS, SYBIL
I am a poet and a picture taker. The panoramic views from Captree State Park inspire both art expressions. This is a truly magical place enjoyed by my family and dozens of other crab catchers who will recognize this picture and share the memories.

DORAN, KATHIE
This is a photo of my daughter. She just learned to climb stairs. I was waiting to see what decision she would make, up or down. I love the look on her face; it was almost a question of should I or shouldn't I? I'm glad I captured this moment.

DOUGLAS-SEVIER, JEANNIE
My son, Shane, was a perfect baby and toddler model. I love the colors in this photo. It was taken at the church playground near our house in Jackson, Tennessee when he was about eighteen months old. This active, happy ham with pretty blue eyes loved to repeatedly go down the spiral slide that he is pictured at the top of.

DRAKE, EMILY A.
"White Mountains" is a picture I took during a trip with my husband, Larry, to visit our son and his family in Mesa, Arizona. Although I have taken many pictures over the years, this is the first photo contest I have ever entered. I have a large family and I enjoy taking pictures of my loved ones too. I like to share my pictures with everyone by displaying my favorite pictures as a continual slide show on my computer. The grandchildren get a kick out of seeing pictures of themselves on the screen.

DROST, ROBERT C.
While playing golf on a local course, I came across a pair of bald eagles building their nest. A few days later, I took my camera to see if I could possibly get a picture of even one of them. I had no idea if I would be successful, but to my surprise, I was able to capture this magnificent bird fiercely protecting its nest. The picture was on display at the clubhouse for several months. Naming the photo was difficult, but one day my wife, June, simply looked at it and said, "Nature's Glory," and that was it!

DROZE, ERIC
Photography has always been one of my greatest passions. Capturing moments, where all the elements converge in a harmonious composition and then sharing them for people to see is what photography is all about for me. "Abandoned" is one of twelve photographs that make up a photo essay I worked on at the University of Iowa. The premise of this photo essay is to capture the feel of a number of rundown rural towns along the Mississippi River in Iowa. This picture encapsulates the ghost town feel I got from many of the small river towns I visited.

DUDLEY, WAYNE
I love shooting with natural light. One day while cleaning my camera, the sun came through the mini blind. I quickly asked a friend to pose for me and this was the magic result. The beauty of photography is that it can magically happen; a gift from the sun and a little creativity!

DUFEK, CRISTINA
My name is Christina Dufek. I love going to my grandparents' cottage in the town of Kazojedy in Czech Republic. My Grandpa's pond is gorgeous and peaceful. I went with my father to see family and had a fun time. I enjoyed my time in Europe over my summer break. I have a pet bird named Ricky who's an African grey parrot. I have a wonderful boyfriend named Ben who helps me out a lot. I have great parents that support me a lot.

DUGGAN, JASON
Throughout life, we all experience moments of searching. Times when we find ourselves looking for answers, guidance, on even purpose in our lives, for some a new career, or a newfound faith, are used as a beacon to navigate the darkness, yet for others, the photographic process can serve as a lighthouse.

DURBIN, ARLENE
"Cloudy Silo" was taken off of a farm road in Nixa, Missouri. I have seen this many times before, but when the cotton ball clouds and beautiful blue sky rolled in, it gave this old fallen barn with attached silo a feeling of a warm sunny day with a much simpler life. I have always had an interest in photography, even taking classes in high school, but I really put my hobby to use two years ago. Nature photography is my favorite and I shoot more photos of that than anything else.

EDWARDS, ROBERT
I took this shot of an open wheel racer battling his way to the 14,110 feet summit of Pike's Peak during the annual "Pike's Peak Hill Climb." I shot both color and black and white, and found the black and white to be more dramatic. Speeds can reach 130 mph on the 12.4-mile gravel course that features 156 turns, 2,000 feet cliffs and no guardrails! The course record stands at 10:04.06. It takes most tourists an hour or more for that same drive! Since 1916, the hill climb is the oldest race in America, second only to the Indy 500.

EGAN, DIANE
This is my favorite photograph of my youngest son, Troy. It was taken at Sandbanks Provincial Park in Picton, Ontario, Canada. In his hand is a water snake he caught while it was swishing through the water. That summer, Troy became an expert snake catcher! It is my personal wish that every child has the opportunity to experience sunshine, freedom, and the wonders of nature.

ELDER, TRACEY
Meet Ashley Ann, my daughter, who is sitting outside on a sunny winter day. She loves the outdoors, especially when we go for rides in her red wagon. She fills my days with laughter and smiles. She is Mommy and Daddy's little angel and our "Bundle Of Joy" too!

ELDREDGE, DEANNA
This is a photo of my children, Joshua and Jenna, apple picking at our annual spot. As they pick the Mac apples and fill up the bag, they take their first bites of the season of the red, shiny, fresh, crisp apples. They enjoy climbing the rocks and running around the apple orchard as well.

ELDRIDGE, MAVIS
Here is my beautiful niece, Alexander Violet Noziska. Even at this young age, she is a ham for the camera. Alexander lives in northern Wisconsin with her parents, Jackie and Rich. She would be the subject of many more photos if she would only sit still! In the meantime, my friend, Don, and I enjoy learning about photography together and challenge each other to do our best. We really love nature and wildlife and like experimenting with different lenses and exposures.

ELLIS, MARVIN ELLIOTT
My community, Miami/south Florida, is a rich reservoir of African diaspora cultures. A primary focus of my photography has been the documentation of the Haitian cultural legacy in south Florida. Papa Guede is a "loa" or spirit of the Haitian Voodoo religion. Guede represents sexuality and death. Guede is characterized by compulsive behavior and speech as he utters obscenities in words and song and performs an erotic dance called "banda." He is always attired in black and wears a high silk hat and dark glasses with the lenses knocked out so that he can view those in his presence so that they don't steal his food. I feel that my photo of Papa Guede captures the true essence of his raison d'etre.

EREKSON, MARIKO GRACE
My photograph was taken when I was eleven years old. I am now thirteen and entered this competition out of complete boredom and thought nothing of it. I never expected it to be published in a book like this. The picture is of my old street right outside my front door. I live on a secluded military base in the Marshall Islands and love taking pictures. I never had much confidence in my photographs, but now I am contemplating a career in photography. I come from a large family of artists, so I have always appreciated art.

ERICKSON, PATRICIA
This is a photo of our son, Emery, who is only a year old in the picture. I grew up loving to take pictures of everything, but it was not until my children came along that taking photos of kids became a passion. I really enjoy using black and white film. It totally changes the whole outlook of your subject. My husband, Matt, and I have two children, Emery and Catherine. We raise cattle and crops in rural Minnesota and wouldn't trade country life for anything. There are so many beautiful and eye-catching images that can be caught on film only in country living. I advise all photography lovers to take a trip and visit rural America.

ESTRADA, MILAGROS
I was traveling on a Disney Cruise and one of the stops was at St. Thomas. We decided to visit so my family and I took a ferry over to St. John. Once there, we took a tour in an open minibus. The driver took us up one end of the island to the highest point and down the other side. This picture was taken during our stop. St. John is a beautiful island. I love taking pictures and felt this was a beautiful view from above looking down at the many gorgeous inlets of St. John.

EWING, GERI
I have always had a passion for the art of photography. One of my favorite sayings is, "Take a pic-

ture, capture a memory." That is exactly what photographs do. There are many moments in life that we want to hold on to forever and photographs enable us to do that. When I saw this small child pick up such a large helmet, oblivious to its size, I had to capture that moment and wonder what thoughts he was having as he walked away.

FAGLEY, HEIDI
A rose suspended in the everlasting moment of now reminds me how amazing the simple things in life really are. That's what photography is about for me. Photography is preserving the individuality in all things, seeing something deeper than what lies on the surface, capturing an emotion with one single press of the shutter, and allowing someone to see something they might otherwise never experience. I am grateful for opportunities to awaken and inspire such moments in others. This is my mother's favorite photo, one I dedicate to the beauty of who she chooses to be in every simple and extraordinary way.

FARLEY, MICHAEL R.
This photo was taken on a path that my wife and I almost didn't take. We seem to capture many wonderful flora and fauna shots in the picturesque state of Florida, but it was fate that hot August day at the Central Florida Zoo.

FELDMANN, WILLIAM L.
This is a photo of my two boys, Billy and Brian. They were eight and four years old at the time. The location was Montauk, Long Island, NY. The camera is a Pentax K-1000 with 100 speed print film.

FINWICK, VERNA L.
In July 2001, I spent three weeks as part of a Medical Mission Team in Nairobi, Kenya. I, as an American Red Cross Instructor, taught First Aid, HIV/AIDS awareness and prevention, and an abstinence program to 400 children in a mission school. The last two days, we enjoyed a brief safari to the Masai Mara Game Preserve. This picture was taken as we drove through the middle of a pride of lions that were enjoying a lazy afternoon siesta. Other than this big yawn, they paid little attention to us. God was good to let me fulfill a lifelong dream.

FIRSING-PARIS, DAWN
We wanted to capture our son's personality and energy. So I put him on his favorite play mat and while he was listening to the music and watching the animals, I was able to do just that. He is our first child and we have another on the way. We love capturing those once in a lifetime moments and showing them to the grandparents!

FLANDERS, GWEN
This is a picture of my nine-year-old son, Ben, playing in the snow for the first time during our Christmas trip to New Hampshire in December 2004. This was the first time the entire extended family had been together in ten years. Everyone joined in the fun of sledding that day: cousins, aunts, uncles, and even Grandma and Grandpa!

FODER, KIM
I made this picture one fine summer afternoon on

the island of Birkholm in the southern region on Denmark. The main motive is the marker for the harbor entrance. In the background, the islands of Egholm and Aero can be seen. I'm an amateur photographer, specializing in photos of nature. I'm living in the southern region of Denmark in a small hatched cottage, far out in the countryside, outside the city of Svendborg.

FOUNTAIN, WANDA JEAN
One chilly evening, I set out with my camera, walking the back road of our rural area home, hoping to capture sunset photos. A cedar bush on my left caught my immediate attention, and with my camera, in that split-second of time, I caught the bursting light of the setting sun in the middle of that bush. Later, the title came to me, "Let Light Shine Out Of Darkness."

FRANKLIN, STEPHEN R.
I love taking my children, Joshua, Chandra, and Nicholas, to the beach with my girlfriend, Marya Merrill, and her children, Joshua, Jake, and Amber, along with my 4.2 mp Toshiba camera. To be able to get such a sight on film is exciting, as I enjoy photography very much. This picture was taken at Moss Beach, California.

FRANTZ, DONALD D.
This photo was taken in early June. A friend and I were supposed to be at a meeting. However, a day this beautiful could not be wasted. So, we took the maid of the mist, and I got this picture at the base of the American falls at Niagara Falls. We missed the meeting, but had the time of our lives.

FRAZER, FAWN
"A Wave In Time" sparks memories of the beach in whoever sees it! Great photos are not always the shots taken with the best equipment. Great photos are the shots that cause the onlooker to turn back time in their own mind! I believe that photographs are our only true means of time travel! This shot could be anyone's fond memories of time spent at the ocean. It could be Martha's Vineyard of summer 2004. But it could also be the shore of NJ, or a shore you remember. It seems I really captured "A Wave In Time!"

FREEMAN, TONYA LENETTE
This is a photo of my niece, Jolean, three months before she turned two years old. The picture was actually taken at one of my other niece's birthday parties. I am in the United States Army so I do not get to visit my family often. However, I actually was home this past year for the birthday party. Jolean came into the kitchen and asked if she could please have something. At that moment she just looked too cute, so that is when I took the picture.

FROST, KELLI
When I take pictures, I am in a completely different world. I am not stressed, worried, or frustrated with anything, it is just the camera, the subject, and me. I am at peace. Nature is just a wonderful photo subject. I believe nature is also very peaceful. This tree is just a tree off the road out in the country west of where I live. This tree to me just represented "A Little Peace Of Nature."

FURTNEY, KRISTA
This is a photo of my daughter, Ashlynd, at eight months. This picture exhibits the personality of Ashlynd perfectly. She is so happy and entertaining. I love this photo! It is amazing how I caught her so perfectly. Usually when I get the camera out, she comes running or crawling towards me and the moment is lost.

GAONA, DELINDA
I have always loved a cloudy sky in the early morning. Having recently purchased a camera, my husband and I took a drive one Saturday to see if I could capture the beautiful morning. As we drove through the grape vineyards of rural Kern County, we came across a creek where I snapped this shot as the sun began to rise. It is always pleasant to wake up each morning to such a scene, which inspired me to title this photo "Amanecer," which is Spanish for "to start the day."

GARAWAY, KAYLA
I called this photo "BFF Twins" because Mia is my BF (best friend) and in university, everyone thought we were twins. The picture showcases the two of us on her nineteenth birthday and the smiles on our faces honestly illustrate how much fun we are having. Like we always say, "Life just wouldn't be fun without each other."

GARCIA, NELSON
On a recent trip to Cuba, en route to the Pine of the Rio Mountains, heading to Caserio de Fierro, I observed two men and a young boy in a typical farmer's transportation driven by two oxen coming down from the mountains. I wanted to capture the beauty of the land and of Jose Fco Valdes, Ramon Reyes, and his twelve-year-old son, Rolandino, who surpass many hard days on the farm. I dedicate this photo to my children, Santy and Raulito Garcia, who helped me select this photo and Joyce Hendley, who helped me with the translation.

GARLAND, LORENE
The scene in my photograph, "Crystal Morning," I see briefly once or twice a year. The camera has to be ready, for when sun warms the scene slightly, the ice crystal effect is gone. I believe that any scene that commands a second look deserves to be captured on film. I always have my camera ready. I'm a landscape artist. I take a lot of scenery pictures for reference for paintings. Sometimes I change the composition around for a painting, and sometimes I paint the scene as it is. My son, Ted, a scuba diver and photographer, enlarged the photograph "Crystal Morning" and suggested that I enter the contest. I'm considering doing a painting of it; that will be a challenge. Thanks for selecting my photograph.

GARMON, TASHA
This photo is of my husband, Billy, with one of our dogs. We try to take a vacation to a beach every year. When I took the picture, I was hoping for a simple picture of my husband playing on the beach. What I got was a beautiful reflection of a perfect gloomy day. The wide-open beaches of Galveston are now our favorite vacation spot. Capturing such a beautiful scene encourages me to keep my camera ready. You never know when the perfect photo op will arise. I love you, Billy, and thank you for always encouraging me.

GARVIN, MARY JO
Ten years ago, we adopted a beautiful Border collie mix, who we named Muttlie. To say that she continually adds much joy and humor to our lives is an understatement! One hot August afternoon, my husband, Jerry, discovered her comfortably sleeping in the poppy patch behind our house. The only evidence as to her whereabouts was a black nose emerging from the foliage and a soft, snoring sound! This photo is one of a series I took as she slowly awakened and realized her cool hideaway had been uncovered.

GAYHART, LINDSAY
This is a photo that I took at my grandparents' cottage on Keuka Lake. I was trying out my new camera that I got for my birthday. I've always liked taking nature photos. I'm going to start college in the fall for photography and hopefully my skills will be improved.

GEARHART, KAREN R.
Penny came to my son, Jeffrey, and me when we needed some happiness in our lives. Penny is a mix of pug and Chihuahua and is now two years old. Her favorite toy is a small stuffed zebra that she plays with all the time. No matter what goes on in the world around her, she is always happy and will forever hold a special place in our hearts. Penny is my little princess, everyone.

GENTRY, BETTY
I have been interested in photography for several years. I am very much an outdoors person who likes to stay involved with nature and my surroundings. I have always been fascinated with the miracles of nature and the beginnings of plants, trees, and animals. I love capturing things with my photos that most of the time we take for granted. This was an expression of my thoughts that made me think of "The Beginning."

GERBER, BRIAN W.
I took this photograph of a great blue heron at a lake in Woodstown, NJ near my home. I wanted to show that you can find beauty anywhere no matter where you live if you just look. I live in a small town but there are always great photographs waiting to be taken.

GILSON, PAUL
Paul Gilson is a professional mechanical engineer registered in Illinois and Indiana who annually attends the Shakespeare Festival in Stratford, Ontario, where the photo was made of the swans on the Avon River. It is very unusual for the swans to approach each other, form a heart-shaped reflection in the water, and for the photographer to have his camera ready for the event.

GOERING, HOLLI
I've always enjoyed taking pictures, but I really got into it after my first child was born in 1984. I wanted my children to always have many memories of every step of their lives. I have acquired countless photos and an album for each year of their lives. I love capturing the beauty of many things. This photograph is of my great-nephew and our bunny. His proud parents are my niece, Rachael, and her husband, Tom. My husband, Karl, and I were baby-sitting that beautiful summer day when we decided to take a picture of this memorable moment.

GRADY, LISA A.
This picture is of my pet bird named Emma. She is a quaker parrot and at the time was six months old. She was ready to brave the wildlife, so I put her in a small oak tree in my front yard. I enjoy taking pictures and I thought the colors blended beautifully.

GRANO, JOSEPH P.
While serving in the U.S. Army in Korea, I have taken the time and opportunity to visit many Asian countries. At the time of this particular photo, my wife was in Thailand and I was in Fukuoka, Japan. There had been a typhoon not two hours prior and I felt a bond with this lone sentinel centered in the background, surrounded by uncertainty. I was feeling a desperate emptiness without my beloved wife by my side and it was a feeling that I tried to fuse into this photo. To my wonderful wife and inspiration in everything I do, Panatda, I can only succeed with you next to me.

GRANT, EVERETT L., JR.
I was born on September 23, 1957 on a dairy farm. I farmed for twenty-five years and now am a dozer operator and a motocross track builder for dirt bikes. I captured this beautiful sundown while dozing on my neighbor's property. I am married with three lovely children, one girl and two boys. We live on a beautiful farm in Cumberland County, Tennessee. I have always heard of the Northern Lights and how beautiful they are. When I saw the colors in my photo, I thought to myself that this has got to be our southern lights. So I named it, "The Tennessee Southern Lights." This is the first contest that I have ever entered and I am really excited. Hopefully everyone can enjoy the true beauty of this photo.

GREEN, DANA
Our daughter, Devyn Isabel Green, was born on February 8, 2004. My husband, David, and I were trying to prepare dinner but Devyn was being very fussy, so we put her in the Baby Born. In just two short minutes, Devyn looked at her daddy and stopped fussing. I could not believe the way our five-week-old little princess was looking at her father. It was as if she was looking at him like he was the most beautiful sight her little eyes had ever seen and instantly fell in love. I could not get to the camera fast enough to take this picture. I feel that it is just priceless.

GREEN, LORRAINE
Sibling love is a beautiful thing. My parents taught us to love each other. I taught my children to love each other. They taught their children to love each other. This picture captures the sibling love that has been passed down through the generations. These are my grandchildren, Ashley and Joshua. We are a very fortunate family.

GRIEME, PEGGY L.
Some years ago, I heard it said, "Photos are win-

dows to the mind!" They not only let others see what we see, but for me, my photos also bring to mind many wonderful memories and feelings. This photo is of my fifteen-month-old grandson, Judah, discovering himself in a mirror. This brings back memories of his dad, Jonathan, and his discoveries growing up. Now I really understand the "grand" in grandparent. It's "grand" to revisit those forgotten memories.

GRINAGE, CAROLINE
I've always loved the fall season. This time of the year always produces such beautiful, bright colors that it almost seems unreal. So, giving this picture a title was no problem at all because this particular season simply speaks for itself. Although fall is an exceptional time in nature, there's only one thing that I don't like about it—it's over with before you know it! I just feel blessed that I was able to have my camera with me to capture fall at one of its finest moments.

GROSS, LISA
Those unexpected moments seem to always make the best pictures and this was one of those moments. While vacationing on the island of Corfu, I saw this little donkey on the side of the road. I went to snap a quick picture when its owner stepped out. I then asked permission to take a picture of her and her donkey. I took the picture, thanked her and waved good-bye. She hopped onto her donkey and trotted away. I knew then that this was going to be one of my favorites.

GROUT, SANDRA
This photo of my two-year-old son, Bryce, and his best friend, Dylan, was taken at the pumpkin patch. I love to take pictures of children just being themselves. I took this one because it was so sweet and endearing how he seems to be leading her. I've found that the best pictures are always not posed. As a first time mother, I've found that my son is my favorite photo subject. I always have my camera ready so I can capture life's little moments.

GRUGNALE, KATHY
I met her at preschool; it was love at first sight. I thought no one could replace Teddy, my teddy bear, but she captured my heart. Here I sit stranded at the altar, my heart broken into a thousand pieces. Thank goodness for Teddy . . . he would never leave me.

GULYAS, ATTILA
I am an amateur photographer with a fairly large portfolio. I have always admired the majestic beauty of predators, especially large cats. All my life, I have dreamt about visiting Kenya, but I have never had a chance to go there. This cheetah caught my eyes when I was visiting the Toronto Zoo. I found her quiet nobility and calm strength irresistible. The image expresses everything I find important in the art of photography as much as in the art of life. I document nature's beauty with humility, respect, and love, capturing the essence of each moment before it passes.

GUTIERREZ, MAIRA
Even since I was a young girl, I have always been an admirer of the natural beauty of our Earth. My father, Higinio Pena, always taught us to enjoy the sky, for it is free and that God was telling us to pay attention and appreciate the beauty of our world. So when I saw the unique formation and colors of these clouds, I just had to photograph them to capture this beautiful moment in time. I am a very proud grandmother of two beautiful little girls, Arabella and Mya. I will surely pass on what my father gave to me. One of the reasons for the beauty of this photograph is that I live with my best friend and husband, Gabriel, in Hesperia, California, where the sky is always blue. We have four wonderful children, David, Michelle, Tommy, and Gabie.

HADDOX, LAYLA
My name is Layla Haddox and I am twenty-four years old. I believe, "Every photo tells a story." I take my camera everywhere I go because there is always a moment waiting to be captured. The photo of mine published in this book is a picture of my four-year-old cat, Salem. He's a talker!

HAESEKER, LINDA M.
I enjoy taking pictures all the time. This photo is a picture of my daughter, Ashley, and her two little friends, Britany and Katelyn, on Halloween. I am always taking pictures on holidays and different occasions. Children seem to love having their pictures taken. I like action shots best of all. I never go anywhere without my camera. Children are the funniest to photograph. I always get double sets of pictures, so I can give them to the children to put in their photo albums. My two daughters both love taking pictures also.

HAGAN, NANCY
Taking pictures with my 35mm is a passion of mine. I rarely go anywhere without it. I'm always looking for that photo op. One afternoon, I went for a walk near the beach. I could hear the waves, but I could not see them. I came upon what was once a fence. I felt the wind brush past me and rush towards the remnants of it. As I was standing there, it was like a moment of the past. I knew I had to take this picture as I was in awe of its beauty.

HALE, BETSY
My husband, Harry, and I love to ride along the ocean, especially after storms. The picture, "The Angel After The Storm," (oh so pretty!) was taken on December 27, 2004. When I took the picture, I saw beautiful bright light filtering through the clouds. Later, when I adjusted the brightness, I noticed this beautiful Angel in the clouds! The Angel seems to mean something to everyone I show it to because it brings tears to their eyes. Maybe it gives them inspiration or it reminds them of a deceased loved one. I really love sharing this with others. Are Angels really watching over us?

HARPER, SHERI
Our son is eleven years old and plays baseball. He was invited to play in Cooperstown, NY at the Cooperstown Dreams Park. We were flying from Las Vegas to New York and while over Nebraska ran into a thunder and lightning storm. I took this picture out of the window of the airplane. I was so excited it turned out the way it did. I love to take pictures and it seems that I miss so many opportunities when they come along. I didn't miss it this time. Thank you for allowing me to share it.

HART, CAROLYN S.
This is a picture of my granddaughter. I watch her every day and love to take pictures of her. I baked a lot of cookies for Christmas this year and got the idea to make her my little helper. Her cute little smile and sweet disposition made this photo turn out so cute. She was six months old at the time of the picture. She really makes my life so much better! I just love her!

HARTIGAN, DENICE
I am so proud that two of my pictures were picked to be published in this wonderful book! It is a great surprise for me! I took some pictures on our trip to Italy! What a beautiful country! My sister, Cristina, and her husband, Mario, live there and invited my husband, Tiru, and me to visit them! It was a trip to remember! See Rome then die . . . that's what they say . . .

HATTEN, ANNA
"Jon David" is a photograph I took many years ago of my dear friend's little boy. Jon is now a man, happily married, and he and his wife are expecting a daughter of their own. Photography has always been a passion of mine. I especially enjoy taking pictures of children and animals. Jon was always so photogenic and this photograph has always been special to me over the years. I am so pleased and honored to share this photograph of Jon in this wonderful book.

HAWKINS, JOHN WALTER
My hobby is digital photography. I enjoy taking photos of main streets in local area small towns.

HAWORTH, DORIS
This is a photo of my four-month-old daughter, Charlize, looking in the mirror. Charlize has a bandana with hair attached to it on her head. I love the expression on her face when she sees herself in the mirror.

HEFFNER, CATHY
Emmitt Kelly Jr. has always been a favorite of mine. He is a silent hobo clown. He does not speak with his mouth, but with his eyes. The problem with that is I cannot hear what he has to say. I can only wonder what he is thinking, what stories he has to tell, what life's lessons he has learned, and what wisdom and knowledge he has to share. I can only wonder.

HEGWOOD, BRENDAN
This is our family's chocolate Lab, Molly. She's full of life and loves to play with us in the snow. In this picture, you can see the true hunter in her. She is one of my favorite subjects because she always likes being center of attention. She brings something very special to our family, and we love her for that. A quote by Roger Caras sums it up perfectly, "Dogs are not our whole life, but they make our lives whole."

HEINECK, DUANE
I have always been the unofficial family photogra-

pher and have dozens of albums to my credit. About three years ago, while I was dealing with multiple health problems, my niece, Kathy Farrow, gave me a beautiful book of photography along with the suggestion that I get involved with photography. I decided that I would enjoy nature and beautiful colorful flowers. I purchased a Nikon N 65, took a course at a local community college, and started my nature interest. "The Red Beauty" was taken at the gardens of the Opry Land Hotel where the lighting was perfect. So far it is my most beautiful work. I am very proud of it and I am pleased that I can share it with so many people.

HENDRIX, JARRED

I love sunflowers and when I saw this huge field last summer, I couldn't resist. It was taken at a game ranch, off the beaten path. I hope you enjoy it as much as I do. I love to take pictures. I am a nineteen-year-old man and I have Down's syndrome. I also love the Special Olympics, like basketball and swimming. I live with my dad, mom, and little sister. She is also one of my favorite photography subjects! Isn't life good?

HERRMANN, SISTER BETH A., O.S.F.

Many years ago, a young Japanese girl, Michiko, stayed for a year at our convent in Baltimore, Maryland, to learn English. Subsequently, she returned to Japan and opened a school to teach English through nursery rhymes. After myriad invitations for me to visit her, I finally accumulated enough frequent flyer miles! Upon arrival, she presented me with a camera, and we went to Kyoto to see shrines and cherry blossoms. The Golden Temple was one of my favorite shots, and having it included in your collection reinforces my belief that God has gifted me with an eye for perspective and beauty.

HERSHBERGER, SHIRLEY ANN

This is a photo of white miniature schnauzers. The photo was taken completely unposed and purely by chance.

HESSON, ESTHER

This is my first great-grandchild, Levi Cooper. His mother, Amanda, placed him in my arms when he was two months old. I was eighty-six and could not lift him. With our eyes, we gave each other a thorough examination. Amanda saw the keen interest and love in our faces and caught it with her camera.

HEWITT, DWIGHT

Children are so much fun to photograph! This is my daughter, Mary Helen. She had just informed me that her baby was sick and she didn't know what to do for her. I placed the phone on the seat beside her and suggested that she call either her mother or the doctor. Her expression was of true concern as she explained her baby's condition in great detail.

HICKS, PATTY

"Little Chatter" or "Chatter bug," as I would often call him, came to me as an orphaned two-week-old baby in need of a mom's TLC. He had to be bottle-fed and nursed back to health. I took this picture of him in his favorite tree, which was also the first tree he ever climbed. Yes, I looked on

proudly and nervously with camera in hand. He went on to make a home with Sandy, another orphaned baby raccoon. In my mind, I can still hear him chatter!

HIGBY, ERIN

This was taken in St. Peter's Square in the fall of 2000. An older gentleman was nearby with uncooked pasta to feed to the pigeons. I was on the Southern Side of the Piazza and decided to head towards the man who was now giving others pasta to attract their own pigeons. I was about halfway to their location when, wanting to remain unnoticed, I bent down and framed this shot. Once mom leaned in, I released the shutter and recorded the moment. Just seconds before, the elderly man had given the boy some pasta and urged a pigeon onto his arm. I've been to Italy a couple times and lived in Rome for several months, but I never saw the pasta man again!

HILL, JANET B.

This photo is of my one-year-old granddaughter and my one-year-old Dachshund. I thought "Sweet Dreams" was a fitting title because of the innocence shown. They are so precious, especially asleep.

HILLMAN, ROBERTA W.

Travel is one of my greatest pleasures. It opens my eyes and mind to see the world around me. Sometimes I'm able to capture the images and moments of places and life. This is a photo of a bride and groom casually strolling along the harbor in Handover, France.

HIRAI, LISA

Sammy is our firstborn child. We waited a long time for him. Now that he is finally here, we marvel at how wonderful he is every second of the day. We're completely in love with this beautiful boy.

HIRSCHMAN, REBECCA

I am seventeen years old and come by cameras naturally through my grandmother, who has it handy at all events. I graduated in June 2005. My training came from a high school teacher of art and photographer, Mrs. Newhouse. In the fall of 2005, I will be off to Morrisville College in New York to start my career in marine biology to become a biologist. They have a great course in photography, which I intend to pick up also. This photo was taken only a mile from my home, at a small stream that always intrigues me when I pass it.

HOERTH, JUDI

I have enjoyed photography ever since I was thirteen. I especially love capturing animals and nature. This is a photo of one of our cats named Angel. He snuck outside somehow and when I looked out the window and saw him eyeing up that ceramic cardinal, I grabbed my camera and shot it from the house so that he wouldn't know I was there. He thought for sure that he was going to be lucky enough to catch that red bird. Watching how intrigued he was made it an interesting sight to watch and capture on film.

HOFFEE, PAM

This is my son, Garrett, experiencing the beach

for the first time. He was just two years old, so I always had my camera handy for moments like this. He and his sister, Abby, just love the feel of the sand and the water. I love to take pictures and I have all my life. Looking at photos takes you back to that moment it was taken so you can enjoy it for a long time.

HOFFMAN, DEONNA

This photo is of my husband, Tim, who has enjoyed being a member of the Corp of Discovery reliving the Lewis and Clark adventures. This was taken at Fort Massac in Metropolis, IL. Tim had been camping on the river for ten days on this keelboat. Our kids, Maranda and Heath, and I have enjoyed the reenacting of the time period of so long ago, 1803-1806. We have learned a lot about the history and have traveled more going on this expedition along the Ohio and Mississippi rivers. What a trip.

HOLZ, KIM

Shortly after I took this picture, the shed was torn down. How lucky I was to capture this image.

HOMJAK, TED

Being outdoor people, each fall, my wife and I go to Benezette, PA to view the elk during the rut. It is amazing to hear the bulls bugle in the valleys. It was late afternoon, we were driving on a state forest road, came over a small rise, and there he was. He had several cows with him. As we arrived, he moved them into the brush. As the bull walked across the small opening, I was able to get the picture with my Canon 545 digital camera.

HOPKINS, EDDIE

This picture of my best friend, Randy, captures the essence of his personality and his ability to bring a smile to the face of everyone he meets. As a nurse in an elderly care facility, Randy brightens the days of the patients on a regular basis. As the youngest of eight children, Randy values family and friends. I consider myself lucky to have met such a genuine and caring person. I love you, Buddy.

HORN, JACQUELINE

When I'm not planting flowers or pulling weeds, I can spend a lot of time with my camera chasing the elusive butterfly. I take all kinds of pictures to capture the moment and am surprised how great some pictures look. My husband and I have been restoring our small four-acre prairie and are happy with the rewards of our efforts. I have used many of my pictures to decorate our home.

HORN, WAYLAND

Thank you for my photo and for showing part of Mineolas' past. What a great place to live.

HOWERTON, MICHELE

This is a photo of my son, Jeremy Tyler, taken when he was one month old. He is our first child and is truly the greatest gift we could have received. I keep a camera in my hand at all times because you never know when a picture-taking opportunity may show up. I'm proud to be able to share our gift with all of you.

HUDDY, KATRINA F.
This is a photograph of two girls with the same first and middle names. They are only a few months apart and both were born in 1999. It was a spontaneous moment that was captured on my digital camera. It was so adorable that they were holding hands. It turned out very well. This photograph is my inspiration to have more fun with my camera and preserve the memories that I capture.

HUNT, JEAN
My husband, Bill, and I live busy lives with work, family, and church activities. We also enjoy traveling and fishing. I am proud of the twenty-five pound eight ounce grouper I caught in the Gulf of Mexico. Bill has worked for twenty-six years as a foreman at a phosphate mine. I have worked in a doctor's office as a bookkeeper for the past twenty years. We have two children, Julie and Sean, and three grandsons, Scott, Michael, and Kameron. My husband and I visited Jekyll Island for the first time when this photo was taken. It is a wonderful place to relax and enjoy life at a slower pace. They also have beautiful sunsets as my picture attests!

HUTCHINSON, LESLEY S. M.
This Christmas shot was simply an opportunity to have some fun trying on a new outfit for Dante's first Christmas. This photo captures well Dante's fun-loving and sometimes even bossy character. The photo's quality, like Dante, was a pleasant surprise. We were expecting a little but then there was the great surprise: one single, beautiful pup, who became the center of attention and has demanded all of family's attention ever since. He loves both people and the camera, as you see! A blend of shih tzu and bichon frise, Dante is definitely one of a kind.

IEZZI, ROSE
This is a photo of a very special little girl, my goddaughter, Gena. I took it as a gift for her daddy for Father's Day. We didn't catch any fish that day, but had one memorable time trying. I enjoy photography very much and will take pictures of almost anything. I live in Bear, DE with my husband, Tom. We enjoy fishing and sports. I would love to do this professionally, someday.

JACKSON, ALDELA C.
I often take a picture with my son. It was the first beautiful picture that I have collected and one of my best. We named him Dominic Kyle. He is a very happy child and keeps on smilin' at this time. We will keep pictures of him forever.

JENNINGS, LYNDA
My daughter, Jules, has always been a camera ham. Even in the midst of a painful mishap, she can turn on that smile in a flash. Jules had stepped on a large thorn and insisted that she needed an ice pack. She was wailing and sobbing about how much her foot hurt, when I grabbed my ever-present camera and said, "Smile!" In an instant, her face lit up and there was her perfect smile again.

JENSEN, MARY ANNE
Nature is my favorite subject. This is a very old barn that was on the property when we bought it.

The pussy willow tree was just starting to bloom, the snow was almost gone, and the pond had trout in it. I like the reflections in water. The tree house in the background was for our grandchildren. We also have deer and wild ducks that visit at times.

JONES, AMANDA ANN
I knew I had gotten lucky when I viewed this picture on my digital camera! I am a fourth-year elementary education major and took this picture during my final internship. I chose to participate with my first grade students in a charity called "Jump Rope for Heart," which is sponsored annually by the American Heart Association. This picture is of a little girl jumping her heart out for a good cause.

KAHLER, LAURA
"How can there be so many different colors in one place?" I remember thinking as I saw these sarongs hanging for sale on the sand in Jamaica. I can visualize the way the wind kept the sarongs moving, almost as if they were flying away. I tried to capture this feeling of energy. These sarongs are works of art themselves, beautifully hand dyed, each one slightly different from the other. As an art teacher, I search for beauty in the world, and this scene was one that caught my eye and made me smile.

KALDENBERG, CASEY
I like to use my imagination while looking at clouds. I am proud of what I've captured on film and so is my family. When they saw this picture, it was all wows. So I am glad to entered it in the contest. Wow, who knew helping bring in the groceries could turn out to be a picture-perfect moment?

KALISHER, CLARE
This is a photo of our firstborn, Benjamin, when he was six months old and had just learned to sit up. I have loved to take photographs ever since I was about seven years old. I dream one day of maybe becoming a children's photographer when my children have grown.

KELLAM, PATRICK JOHN
Eleven-year-old Patrick Kellam took this photo on Mother's Day in 2003. Patrick has wanted to be a firefighter since he was two years old. Whenever possible, he hangs out with and trains with local firefighters. This is the first house fire he saw up close and personal. As you can imagine, it left a lasting impression.

KELLY, JAMES
This is from the Indian Summer Powwow in September 2003. "Wahsutat'ati" means night or darkness in the Oneida language. I was waiting for men's traditional dancer to finish when the fireworks started. I was thinking about fireworks, "Fireworks, what can I do with fireworks?" My heart and brain started working. "How much film do I have? How many shots do I have in my camera? What shutter speed do I use?" The Bussel was hanging on a tripod when I was walking from one side of the arena to the other, as the dancers were completing their category.

KEMP, JASON
I believe every photograph has a story. Whether this swing was a home run or not is irrelevant. What is important is that everyone will remember Sammy Sosa and his home runs for a long time to come. Another thing I will remember about this game, other than capturing this photograph, is the good times spent with my dad, my brother, and a few good friends at a Chicago Cubs game in Wrigley Field.

KENOYER, NIKKI
This is a photo of my six-month-old son, Ethan. He got his first tooth this day, so I went and bought him an ice cream cake. He loved it and I could not resist snapping a photo of this face covered in icing.

KNOP, JAN
I dedicate "Winter In Greenwich Village" to my wife, Justyna Gaweda, the only true love of my life and my inspiration in everything I do.

KOENEMANN, KIM
Brutus was found abandoned, walking the streets of Newark, NJ, at six weeks old. When I took this picture, he was four months old and I just had him sit and look up at me. When he isn't posing for pictures, Brutus enjoys spending time with the pet cat and rabbits, taking naps in the sun on the patio chair, and going for rides in the pickup truck, where he often gets treats from people that he meets. He also enjoys training at obedience school and spending quality time with his boxer girlfriend, Bailie. He earns his keep by bringing in the newspaper and mail (and he once even brought in the phone book). Every night before going to bed, he brushes his teeth (of course, with the help of his owner). Brutus is a very happy and special dog and is adored by many people.

KOHLER, WILLIAM C.
The sizzlers in the photograph range from age sixty-six to seventy-seven. They perform with the California Sizzlin' Seniors in Motion entertainment troupe. My wife, Marilyn McCabe-Kohler, far left in photo (age seventy-five), is the Ms. Senior California Pageant Director. The Sizzlin' Seniors in Motion is the entertainment arm of this program. The sizzlers represent senior women who have reached the age of elegance, sixty years old or more. My camera is always ready to capture the talent, beauty, and charm these performers bring to the senior audiences.

KONEV, HIONIA
This beautiful photo of my view is where I live now. I always think it's so special to live there and enjoy it. Since I see it every day, I don't think much about it. Then when you stop and look at it, it's like seeing it for the first time. It's just the most beautiful view you have ever seen. I just want to share the photo with everyone out there.

KOZMA, BOB
This photo was taken on Big Lake in Maine. I've been fishing up here for years. The story behind this special loon, from a local claiming, is that it had lost its mate and had become friendly with fisherman. So while fishing this lake, we saw a loon in the distance and wondered if the

story was true. We caught a small fish and sloshed it in the water to get the loon's attention. He went under and surfaced a few feet from our boat. I was able to take pictures and enjoy a rare experience with nature.

KRASNER, BARBARA R.
Do you remember the day when the four of us explored the gardens at Chanticleer and discovered an awesome beech tree framed by a sunlit arbor? I took a snapshot and grandpa hung it on his office wall. His patients liked it a lot so he entered it into a contest. The selection committee thought it looked pretty good too. They are publishing that arbor in Chanticleer in a book called "Endless Journeys." I remember that summer day when we set out for Chanticleer Gardens on one of our endless journeys.

KRAUSE, FAITH
My husband and I love photography. We enjoy landscapes and nature and found this rare find when a young coyote crossing the road had stopped traffic at the north rim of the Grand Canyon. As he moved into the woods, he stopped briefly to look back and I was able to capture him in this wonderful picture. Keeping our camera ready has given us wonderful opportunities in nature.

KRUMBEIN, DEL A.
This is a photo of a very intelligent and photogenic Pembroke Welsh Corgi named Winston. Whenever I get out a camera, he is right there to have his picture taken. I have taken many really neat photos of Winston. He is not only my pet, but also my very best friend. He goes everywhere that I go, including the bank, the barbershop, the grocery store, and the post office. When I had my landscape business, he went on the job with me almost every day. Everywhere we go, people think he's really cute and he gets a lot of attention and treats.

KUHLENBECK, ROLAND
Nature fascinates me. After a severe storm approximately twenty-five years ago, the sun popped out and I grabbed my 35mm camera and snapped this shot. The picture has not been enhanced in any way. This is a cloud with the sun shining through it. It looked like a fire from the heavens. I'm saving some more choice photos for the next contest!

KUZNIK, CRYSTAL
This picture was taken on our back porch, where our cats, Tinkerbell, Minnie, and Jazmine enjoy watching birds. We taught them the word "Birdie," alerting them to when birds were at the feeder. When we started to attract squirrels and chipmunks, "Birdie," started to be used for any animal that found its way to our porch. I've always enjoyed taking photographs, mainly of animals and nature. I would like to thank the love of my life, Erik, for always believing in me, and for his reaction when I told him that my photo had become a semi-finalist in this contest.

LAAKKONEN, MARGARET A.
I was drawn to Arizona because of its mystical beauty, leading me to have a healing experience.

LAI, KEAM-MAR
My cat was running and jumping around and then decided to sit on the coffee table next to the bonsai and blanket. Luckily, I had a camera. I love this picture, because the objects came together well as a jungle. Even the glass coffee table looks like a river stream. Bagheera is a name I got from the Disney classic, "The Jungle Book." The panther's name was Bageera. My ex-girlfriend and I raised him as our own. He is my first cat and I miss him so much. This is for you, Bagheera. RIP.

LAKE, KATHY
I am a northern California native who fell in love with the Colorado Rockies as a young girl on a family tour to New York. Almost thirty years later, my dream to live here materialized when Christopher and I pulled up stakes and transplanted my wallpapering business to the beautiful acreage at Slate Rock Ranch, near Bellvue. We've nestled in with our five horses, two dogs, and this very photogenic native Colorado kitty, Brodie. Life here is the ultimate, where the skies are blue, the clouds are dramatic, and if you don't like the weather, just wait a few minutes!

LAMMEY, BRIAN
He soars above me, with some old school tricks. I would like to thank him, Mr. Myers, and Rachel. I wish to continue to love my photography at Hallmark Institute in Massachusetts. Then I would like to become a professional photographer for "Thrasher," but until then I'm going to enjoy having fun with my friends. Follow your dreams, don't follow failure, or turn around.

LANDERS, WENDY
This is the first watermelon I have ever grown by myself. My family had recently moved into a new house. I had dug a new garden. So I tried to grow a new plant, which I loved, but had never grown. I have been a photographer for a year. I have a master's degree in applied social research from the University of Michigan. My hope is that my photography will help me communicate with others more clearly. Photography has helped me chronicle my own life.

LANE, JONATHAN
I am seventeen years old, living in Islington in London. I really enjoy traveling, particularly to exotic and less visited places. I took this photo about a year ago and I liked it because the doorway fitted nicely into the film. I liked the blend of colors turning from brown to green. I like photography, as you can bring something back with you which enables you to show people what it's like and get a feel for a place or country. I try to enter competitions, as in the future, I hope to go professional.

LANGE, RHYAN C.
I have been an amateur photographer for two years. I usually like to take pictures of landscapes and birds. This photo was taken in Words End State Park in Pennsylvania. I took this photo because I saw the beauty of the water and how it is vital to the existence of life. I wanted to share it with friends and other people.

LAPPE, JEAN
Fielder-Jean, the house cat, loves the Christmas tree. She was the runt of the litter, chosen by a softball teammate that is very ill with mix-connective tissue disease. In the beginning, I wanted my friend to choose a healthier cat, but with tender loving care, Fielder-Jean became a soft, beautiful, longhaired cat. In return, the cat is always there for her, cuddling and consoling my friend during her days of rest. Fielder-Jean, once a runt, is now that "Special Gift" that may very well be an angel in disguise.

LARKINS, ANDREA
One afternoon, I took my three kids down to the park for a few pictures. After two hours of trying to get them to all smile at the same time or even alone when it was their turn seemed impossible. On the way back to the car, I realized I didn't have a good picture of Bradley. I asked him to sit for one more picture. He rolled his eyes and sat on a rock near the pond. I snapped a few pictures and we were off. To my surprise, it was the best picture of him ever.

LASTER, PENNY
I love animals, especially horses and living on a farm. I'm a country girl at heart. I also love photography. I'm always taking pictures. My dream is to open a photography studio catering to people with pets. In this photo, Black Jack is two days old. He's the third colt from a mare named Gypsy. The first one was a bay, the second one was black and white, then came Black Jack. It was extremely difficult choosing the perfect picture, because I have several very good ones and this one speaks volumes. The stance of this newborn is so curious and proud. He's looking as though he's saying "Look at me, I'm special."

LE VAN VALKENBURG, NANCI
I have always loved painting and photography. I was bored and so I experimented with light, added flowers from the garden and was amazed with the result. I got my 35mm camera out of the closet and captured my light paintings on film. I have been experimenting and adding other things into the light for six months and enjoy the different creations that I come up with.

LEAVITT, STACIE J.
They say you have to kiss a lot of frogs before you find your prince. This is my eight-year-old daughter, Kayli-Susan. Since she has been able to walk, she has enjoyed frogging in our pond. She loves to kiss them and it is never a surprise to find a frog or two peeking out of her pant pockets. Kayli and my son, Jesse, play for hours either catching frogs or capturing bugs.

LEDFORD, WM. F., SR.
Photography became a necessity in the mid-forties when I joined my father in the publication of his community newspaper and I got into it cold turkey, never guessing that I would someday regard the exercise as a most rewarding side venture. My eye has been trained to some degree to watch for subjects such as "After 9/11." Coming up only days following the disaster, I couldn't pass it by. The dilapidated structure usually carries Georgia Bulldog messages. It was not diffi-

cult for the owners to give way to this consideration of the disaster.

LEE, JENNIFER L.
I have taken thousands of photographs in my life and I have only a handful that makes me say, "Wow!" This is one of them. This photograph is of my children, Lucinda (age three) and Jonathon (age one month). After Jonathon had finished eating, I laid him down to rest. His sister laid down next to him and I thought, what a beautiful moment; I hope I can capture this on film, and voila!

LEGGE, TERRY P.
This little girl was on a field trip with her classmates at Castle Howard in North Yorkshire, United Kingdom. It was in May and a blistering sixty-five degrees. Sunscreen and a popsicle helped prevent heat exhaustion! I guess it's all relative.

LEWELLYN, KAREN Y.
This is a photo of my daughter, Carsyn Lynn, holding a leaf for the first time. She was six months old at the time and studied that leaf for quite a while and then looked up and I snapped the picture. It's one of my favorite pictures of her. I hope she enjoys nature and being outdoors as much as I did growing up.

LINDE, TONI
This is the first photograph that I developed and printed by myself while taking a photography class. I had also just learned how to use the settings on my camera correctly so I was pretty excited when it all came together to get this shot! I have a great teacher!

LOAYZA, ARTURO R.
A particular stranger hitches a ride while taking a swim in a customer's pool. They say to watch out for these particular strangers, because from time to time they wander off to explore creation. Exploring creation to this particular stranger, I would have assumed he got lost. A favor for a favor, I guess he didn't seem to mind. Back you go where you once began, a new step, a new hope. Should you ever come back and I'm there with poise, this time stay away from those cruddy leaves because I can't see down there very well.

LONG, RICK
There are some things in the world that have to be timed just right in order to appreciate the full worth. This is a sunset on the Connecticut River. I consider this photo an example of my major life philosophy, to slow down and take in life. It also shows why I keep my camera close at all times; sometimes a moment may slip by unnoticed.

LONG, STEPHANIE
I took this picture the day my husband, Michael, and I took our son, Jacob, home from the hospital. They fell asleep on the couch and I couldn't help but stare. He was just so perfect, ten little fingers, ten little toes, and his tiny body fit just so between our arms, like we were custom-made for each other. He gets bigger every day and seldom sits still for more than a moment. At least he will always have this moment frozen in time to cherish forever.

LUNDY, MATTHEW
Hi, my name is Matthew Lundy and I'm the photographer for "Sunset On Chain Lake." I took this photo up at my grandpa's cabin in Eagle River, Wisconsin located on Chain Lake. When I took the photo, I was out fishing on the lake and happened to take my camera along. I photographed the sunset, which is strange because I usually photograph the wildlife out on the lake, but the picture turned out well and I'm happy. The best part is that my photo gets to be published in a cool book with other people's photos.

MACK, BENJAMIN CASIMIR
This was a beautiful time in my life when exploration and introductions to new places and people was a personal requirement. After spending the Easter holiday in Palermo, Sicily, my friend, Eric, and I decided to take the hour-long bus trip to the town we'd only heard about in the "Godfather" films. Ah, yes, Son Corleone. I have to say that the experience was something I will never forget, and the people we met were as real as life gets.

MAGOWAN, JUDITH L.
Every October, our son, Danny, carves out a pumpkin with his son, Zachary. They happened to be at our house when I took this photo. They are both very artistic and each year they carve out a very different face. I love to take pictures and I couldn't resist the look on our grandson, Zachary's, face as he looked deep into the lighted pumpkin. It was as though it was whispering to five-year-old Zachary saying, "I See You."

MALDONADO, MANUEL
I love my country, Puerto Rico. It is a beautiful island. When I look around, the history becomes alive and I want the world to remember. I am not a professional; I just love my country. For another detail in my picture, look at the sky and you will see the wonder of the nature. You will see a horse in the clouds.

MALKOSKI, KRIS
Our son, John, received his first car as a Christmas present. He was quite excited and began jumping up and down, over and over, as he took his first spin. His hair became so full of electricity from hitting the top of the car roof that it literally stood on end. Now I wonder what he'll do when he's sixteen and gets his second set of wheels!

MALONE, RICKY
Thank you, but the good Lord created this scene; I just transposed it to paper for him!

MARQUEZ, RICH
I came to Clear Lake a year ago to renovate my sister's house on the lake thinking I would be done by Christmas. I was wrong about which Christmas. "Sunrise At Sunrise Shores" is my view of the lake every morning when I wake up. I'm thankful for this opportunity to share.

MARSHALL, LORI ANNE
I love taking pictures of my kids. Most people gasp when I tell them how many picture files are stored on my hard drive! When I saw the look on my daughter, Lilly's, face in this photograph, I thought to myself, "She's so little and innocent."

It has been one of my favorites ever since. I have another daughter, Emma, who is seven years old. Between her and my husband, Rory, I have all the help I need to keep Lily innocent as long as I can.

MARTIN, MICHAEL
Youngs Vineyard is just one of many beautiful sights I see every day in Amador county. When I first moved to Plymouths to care for my mom, Betty, I never imagined I would find a hobby that allowed me to show so many people the grandeur of this area. Beauty and California Gold Rush history is all around me. Riding with me in my little red Toyota is Marty. He and I will continue to record and preserve history through photos like this one.

MARTINEZ, AMANDA SUE
My son, Wyatt, was born six weeks early. He spent a week in the N.I.C.U. I took this picture when Wyatt was a month old when he was in the hospital for a blood transfusion. The doctors don't know where his blood went, but it's been staying normal ever since. I thank God for my sweet baby. I know angels are watching over him every day.

MARTINO, AL DI
I acquired an interest in photography when I was twelve years old and maintained my own home darkroom. I enlisted in the U.S.N. in 1947 and graduated from USN Aerial Photography School in 1948. I continued my Aerial Photography duties until 1952, when I was honorably discharged. I did no photography for several years. In the late 1980's, I acquired a new interest in photography and have been enjoying it ever since. "Dragonflies" was shot with a Cannon Clan II with a Tamron 28 - 300 zoom lens.

MASTERS, GARY
This is a photo of my first visit to Spain. I'm a nature lover and I take few photos of people, but I have many of the natural surroundings of places I've been. This particular photo still takes my breath away as I remember standing on top of the mountain viewing the Mediterranean as it crashed into cliffs jutting out from Formentor on the island of Majorca, Spain.

MATERA, LAURA M.
It was my first visit to the Grand Canyon and it was a vacation I will never forget. My sister and I took the sunset tour to see the canyons in a different perspective. Everyone on the tour was admiring the beautiful sunset ascending on the canyons. I walked a little farther than the others and came upon this magnificent sight! The silhouette of the desert trees in the sunset was breathtaking! It looked like people reaching up to the heavens! Hopefully I captured what I was feeling. I hope you enjoy this picture as much as I do!

MAY, ANTHONY
I was on my honeymoon testing out my new camera. When I came across this beautiful flower, I had to stop to take a photo. I had no idea it would come out so good.

MAYNARD, DARLA
The feeling of flying hundreds of feet over the

ocean, legs dangling in the air, wind blowing through your hair, hearing nothing but birds because you're so high above the water: parasailing, there's nothing like it. The pure look of excitement on my mother's face sums up her experience parasailing for the first time on a recent trip to Cabo San Lucas, Mexico. This is a photo I'll always treasure because the look of joy on my mom's face brings a smile to mine.

McCARTNEY, SUSAN

My husband, Irving, and I have been snapping photos of our first child at every opportunity. I guess it is that new parent syndrome. This photo was taken when Darla was nine months old. She was playing with a cookie tin lid and appeared to be exercising. We did not realize what we captured on film until this photo was processed. Her reflection in the lid was captured by chance. We are truly mesmerized by Darla and love trying to capture special moments on film.

McFADDEN, LINDA

I'm known as resident photographer/historian amongst family and friends with my camera in hand at family gatherings, friends' parties, and other events. Even the basset hounds can't escape my beloved hobby! I'm keen on framed picture groupings and scrapbooks. My six- and eight-year-old granddaughters, Mackenzie and Taylor, have also been bitten by the bugs!

McGARIGAL, ELLEN

Who says having MS and being physically challenged will stop you from doing what you love? I have been in a wheelchair for six years now, and still enjoy taking lots of photographs. This deer came right up to my kitchen window, just like many other wild animals. I love this photograph because it brings back memories of my old house in Rangeley, Maine. My handicap has not yet stopped me from doing what I love most, and I hope that this will encourage people like me to try and follow their dreams. Moments captured will last a lifetime.

McLAUGHLIN, LISA

This picture was taken on a family vacation with my husband, Brian, and our son, Gage. We were visiting Brian's grandparents in Naples, FL, where they reside in the winter. Whether from the pier or the beach, residents and visitors alike make it a point to enjoy these spectacular sunsets. Normally we forget to take pictures, but we were lucky enough to capture this moment on film.

McLEAN, CAROLYN D.

Morning at Owlshead, Maine captures a vacation memory of a sunny June day: a gentle rippling of the water at the shore, a whiff of salt air, the visit to Owlshead light behind us, and the incredible luck I had photographing the lights and shadows of the scene.

McNATT, VERNA

After retiring from the Corps of Engineer in Tulsa, Oklahoma twelve years ago, I enjoy annual cruise vacations to eastern and western Caribbean, Mexico and Alaska, not to mention, trips to Seattle, Vegas, New York, etc. I've found great pleasure in video recording my trips; also, I carry my 35mm camera for colorful pictures for my many albums. That has become a fun hobby I can take with me wherever I go and share with others. The "Sunset, Inside Passage" photo was taken during one of my trips to Alaska on the beautiful Alaska State Ferry "La Conte." The scene was shot somewhere between Juneau and Sitka (my hometown).

MEARS, LAURA

This is a photo of my dog, Duke. He is a golden retriever. Duke enjoys running and playing at the beach, and he is very photogenic. Duke has always been my favorite subject. Best of all, he never complains about being the center of attention. Duke is my best friend and companion.

MELIA, BARBARA

I have loved to take photos for a hobby for many years. I am a volunteer at an animal rescue group called Catales Inc., so I have many wonderful subjects to photograph. Roseanne was pleased to pose for this one.

MENSCH, BARBARA

The elegance of nature's grays, the soft, warm, shiny coat of feline fur, the rough bark of the pussy willow tree, the cloudy autumn sky and the shiny frosted leaves, are all the grays preceding winter's whites. The colors nature provides, the hues, the blends, and the shades, fascinate me. Photos with both animate and inanimate objects provide contrast within the infinite nature of our world we often overlook. My camera and I are traveling a path, with nature as our guide.

MICHAEL, KATHY

I couldn't resist taking this photograph! One afternoon I called my mother, Janet Bradshaw, to help me create the picture I had envisioned in my head for years. We filled a basket with towels, made Trent a slingshot and tied Brooke's hair back. Last but not least, we hung Erika from the clothes line in our backyard. After each photo, my mom would run and rescue Erika from her hanging! After several pictures, I finally took this one and loved it! (Lucky for Erika!) Every time I look at this picture, I can't help but smile!

MICKELBORO, VERA

One day, while traveling through Campton, New Hampshire, I stopped to snap this photo after a snowstorm. I love taking pictures of nature, because God's creation is so beautiful. Photography is one of my favorite hobbies. It's fun to compete in local fairs, too.

MILEWSKA, KAMILA

On September 11, 2001, I lost my only brother. He was only twenty-one and he worked in the World Trade Center. After that, I was very depressed and I didn't want to live anymore. Then something amazing happened, I got pregnant and my daughter, Maya, was born. She is two years old now. She gave me strength and hope. She is God's sign that life must go on. When I'm watching her, I can see my brother's spirit. I took this picture because the look of joy on Maya's face is something that keeps me going.

MILLER, KARA

This photograph, "Twilight Beach," was taken while on a vacation to Miami, Florida. In this view of Matheson Hammock Park, I wanted to capture the true body of the sun setting over Biscayne Bay. My interest and passion for photography began while I was in college pursuing a degree in Graphic Design. Many of my photographs have become special gifts for family and friends, as I endeavor to transform my photography into an artistic statement.

MILLER, THELMA K.

Here are two hardworking young men hard at work doing a dirty job, but enjoying each other's company. They are my grandsons, Japaul and Jacob Rockwell, of Wakeman, Ohio. I have always been interested in photography and now and then take one I really like and enjoy. This is one of those pictures. I have been painting in watercolors and acrylics for about fourteen years and enjoy this hobby also. Before that, I was a commercial pilot and flight instructor for forty-eight years and before that, I was a Women's Air Force Service Pilot (WASP), and one of America's first military pilots.

MOBLEY, AILEEN

This picture was taken at the airport in Maryland. Our first great-grandchild, Zachary, was a little two-year-old red-haired boy with a joyous disposition and laughing green eyes. If you asked him, "How are you, Zach?" his reply would always be, "I'm fine." He is now a very serious twelve-year-old. He is a good student with a kind heart, always thoughtful of other people. He has a great talent for writing and is knowledgeable of world problems. He has a wonderful family of his parents and ten-year-old sister.

MOLLISON, TOM

Hello, my name is Tom. I'm fourteen years old, and I love spending my summers traveling the back roads, and taking pictures with my grandfather, who I call P paw. I got hooked on photography a year ago, when my great uncle and photography buff, Bob Tibbets, said I had a "photographer's eye." On my Spray Falls trip, I applied the basics of photography, but I was still learning the tricks of the trade. I was just leaving Spray Falls when I glanced back and noticed an interesting photo opportunity. I snapped the shot, and here it is today, in a book!

MOLNAR, JUDITH

At a family reunion, I had been watching my two-year-old grandson, Grant, entertaining himself with his lawn mower. He went back and forth with such concentration that he seemed oblivious to everyone around him. He adores his dad and mimics him any way he can. He even carries his own keys like his dad. I took the picture because I wanted to capture Grant's intense focus on being grown up . . . "Just Like Dad."

MONET, KRISTI

This is a photo of my willow tree taken during an ice storm. I love to take very unique photos that capture the eye. Living in the country, I have things to photograph all the time. My collection just keeps growing. I am an artist and love to sketch and paint landscapes as well.

MOORE, SHANNEN MARIE

This is a photo of my pup and me. Yogi, my dog, and I are just sitting in the living room. It's a picture that goes well with the man's best friend theme. Yogi is and always will be my best friend.

MORENO, JOSE L.

Jose has specialized in making Fuji and Polaroid instant prints for the last fifteen years. He is creating and composing without any formal training or rules to explore the inspiration of the new age.

MORITZ, COLLEEN

This is a photo of my oldest grandson, Keith Downer, then nine, of Rochester, NY. We were all making snowmen in my yard; however, Keith who is artistic and has a sense of humor, decided to make his a kangaroo. After he had finished and leaned on it as if he was asking the kangaroo, if it's "Too Cool For Joey," I had to take the picture. I try to take photos of my grandchildren in special situations. This one won out. We're so happy we chose it.

MORSE, STACEY ELIZABETH

This is my seven-year-old daughter, Sadie. She received the guitar for Christmas from her grandfather and his soon-to-be wife. She loves to teach herself and she especially loves to play for others. Sadie sings and puts on shows for our family.

MOSSER, JESSICA

I have always loved looking at and taking pictures. I always keep a camera near me. I started with film and now I am learning how to do digital. Keeping a camera near me is how this particular picture came to be. I saw the cat on the porch and thought it looked good, so I shot it. I see now I made the right choice. I have only done some summer college courses as far as my education goes. I have done some local work. Mainly I do dance photography, but I like a lot of other things too. I am currently moving to New York City to pursue my career.

MOUNTS, MARJORIE A.

We have always had cocker spaniels. Little Honey is our sixth. Since both our son and daughter grew up with pets, they now have cockers, too. Angel is our daughter's pet, our granddog. The girls love each other and were lying together in the sunlight. I was surprised that they both cooperated and posed so sweetly, but then they are both the best puppies ever! They are a source of unconditional love and never-ending joy to us. Life without our Little Honey would be totally unimaginable.

MYERS, RIDGELY

This photo of our son, Connor, was taken while playing at Audubon Zoo in New Orleans. Connor loves to play with his "girlfriends," Allee and Cassidy, and we often get them together for play dates. As this photo shows, Connor always has a great time! You can really feel his excitement and energy in this picture, which is one of the reasons I love it so much! The other reason: he's as cute as can be!

NEAL, TARIS ANN

This is a photo of my son, Tayvon. He was eighteen months old in this picture. It is my favorite picture of him. He was giggling while he was eating a cookie. To me, this picture captured the most beautiful look on his face, a look that will forever be in my mind. I have stared at this picture for hours, thanking God for the most gorgeous gift that has ever been given to me in my life.

NEWELL, KAY L.

Boomer was a three-year-old Tundra Wolf that I raised since he was three weeks old.

NEWLAN, ELAINE

I love to capture color in my pictures. This is a photo of a sunrise taken at Virginia Beach, VA while on vacation with my mother, Ann. I love to travel with my husband, Rex, when we can. We own five golden retrievers that are our kids. I want to thank my friend, Patty, for talking me into entering my photo. I am so thankful that my love for nature will be shared with others.

NICHOL, JUDITH A.

Snuggles is what I call my throwaway kid with an attitude. She was abandoned at the age of six weeks. She was either injured at birth or has a birth defect, as she cannot meow; however, her ability to hiss and growl works very well. Until she was de-clawed, every time she wanted attention, she would climb up my pant leg.

NICHOLS, DOYLE

This photo of BJ was taken while he was waiting for his food. He knew he had to be calm. Normally BJ is one active poodle! I have been taking photos of pets and family for several years. This one appealed to us for his serious look. We hope to share it with many!

NICOLLS, KAREN

This is a quiet moment of my grandson, Gregory Donald Nicolls, with his great-uncle, Bob Sweeney, feeding ducks at the lake on a beautiful sunny afternoon. This photo is one of my favorites; it will add to my wall of family photos, which is quite large.

NIELSEN, LYLE

We live on Sand Lake about three miles from the town of Moose Lake, Minnesota. My wife was recovering from cancer. From her bed, she could see the lake through her window. One morning, she said, "Lyle, hurry, take a picture of the beautiful sunrise." I rushed out and took the picture with an Instamatic camera. I am a retired pastor and was home taking care of my wife.

NIEMUTH, MATTHEW CHARLES

This picture of a sunrise near Waupaca, Wisconsin was taken with plain old 35mm camera. I have always been interested in how the weather works and affects our lives. I have been studying and reading about the weather since I was eight years old. I'm twenty-three years old. My birthday is on June 11. I'm from Waupaca, Wisconsin, where I was born and raised. My hobbies and things I do for fun are fishing, walking, swimming, anything outdoors, photography, reading, studying and learning about meteorology. I like to share the

pictures that I take with my family members, some of the employees at my work, people at the National Weather Service in Green Bay, Wisconsin, friends, and other people that I know. I get very good complements on the pictures that I share with them.

NOFERI, BETH ANN

I had spent four years of my life as an art major at Ivy League Cornell University. I had taken studio fine arts and studio photography courses. Having been in a sorority with many friends, I was lucky enough to have one of my girlfriends offer to pose for a photo shoot. In college, I took many photos of the downtown Ithaca area, events at the college, and photos of my friends. I feel that this is the best one I took of my friend, Lee, in upstate Ithaca, New York.

NOROTSKY, JENITA B.

I wanted to capture a picture that was symbolic and inspirational. The Lord told me to look up and take the picture. This is the result. Lighthouses represent towers of majesty and strength, yet they are caring and loving enough to guide ships and vessels safely to shore. Matthew 5:16: "Let your light so shine before men that they may see your good works and glorify the Father in Heaven." This reminds me of the call. 2000 is the address of Montauk Point Lighthouse. We have bumper stickers that read "Montauk, The End." Actually, it's the beginning.

NOWATKOWSKI, CHERYL

This is one of the five raccoons that started coming to our home when they were babies. As they got older, they made themselves very comfortable. I love to take pictures just for fun and the animals that run around my home are easy to snap. It brings me great joy to be able to share them with others.

NUSS, BEV

At two-and-a-half years old, this picture captured Griffin showing signs of following in his Papa and Dad's footsteps. His dad had to give him timeout at first from the hammer; he gets mad if we try to substitute toy tools. Hopefully, one day he will be wearing the pouch around his waist with a two-year-old assisting him.

O'REILLY, PAULINE NAN

This is my baby cat, Miyu, at just nineteen days old. My whole life has changed with her. She would sleep with me and wake up with me until now. When she opened her eyes, the first thing she saw was me. Miyu takes baths and showers with me every day and even enjoys soaking in the hot tub . . . must be a Japanese cat. She even waits for me at the door every day at 5:30 p.m. and stays there until I come home. I don't think she knows she's a cat; she probably thinks she is a hairy human. I am proud to say she is in good health and has grown up to be just like me. Miyu has made my world complete.

OLSON, ROXY

I have been taking pictures since I was about eight years old. I like to take photos of flowers, birds, animals, insects, and even an occasional frogorsnake. My favorite medium is the sky, whether it is a sunset, a rainbow, a stormy sky, or an unusual cloud formation. It's amazing how beautiful the sky can be.

OTTOSEN, KRISTI
"The Burn" was taken during a control burn for the Amery Fire Department. The Fire Department uses the control burns as practice. Being the wife of one of the captains of the Amery Fire Department, I have many opportunities to take many awesome pictures. "The Burn" is just one of many.

PADDOCK-ZIMMERMAN, JEANIE
A small black and white camera was presented to me on my eleventh birthday in 1954. Much to my family's chagrin, nothing escaped the lens of that camera within a quarter of a mile radius of the farm where I was raised. I continued to torture them through the years with everything from that first camera to present-day camcorders and digital cameras. After spending most all of my adult life in the east San Francisco Bay Area in California, the return to my roots in Kansas has opened my eyes to the many, many beautiful scenes of the Heartland. And, much to my delight, I am capturing God's canvas creations without disdain or disfavor from my subjects!

PALESOTTI, JENNIFER
"A Pure Jewel" is a perfect description of my six-year-old daughter, Sydney. She shares the spotlight at our home with her twin sister, Savanna, and loves her three mini-dachshund pups. My passion is photography, and to capture the true personality of a child as my prize.

PALFI, BILL
Thank you for your kind words, I cannot wait to see the picture in a book. Win or lose, I aim to improve my images, because there are in nature so many stories not yet told. I hope to tell some of them with my camera, like the eagle taking that fish to his three babies and mate, until one day the hunter hopped from tree to tree with father behind and a final big leap that ended with all of them soaring high in the sky.

PALKOWSKI, DONNA
I looked in awe one January evening at a star whose cheerful sparkling lit and colored a cold night sky. That twinkling one became my very own wishing star. "Flap like a bird, jump like a fish, stand up, sit down, wish-wish-wish," once stated by the very famous Winnie the Pooh, himself. Ryan Anthony was born on January 13, 2003 in Milwaukee, Wisconsin. Every night I thank that twinkling wishing star for my most important wish come true, my nephew, Ryan, in my life!

PALMER, JACQUELINE
The look of innocence in a child is priceless and pure as a lily of the valley. This portrait of my daughter, Julia Lynette, was taken after her dance recital. Julia is little sister to her three older brothers, Nathan, Andrew, and Zachary. She has been a blessing to me. I will have many precious moments to reflect on her childhood memories in the years to come. Children are truly a blessing from God. I work as a school nurse and enjoy photography, especially of family events and

nature scenes. Our family lives in the small town of Dansville in upstate New York.

PANNONE, MELBA
This photo is an example of the creative and artistic way that I look at things. This accident took place right in front of me. I was on my way to Georgia, traveling on highway 301 in north Florida. I drove a safe distance away and took some photos, just before the truck and car exploded. This one was the most interesting. My granddaughter, Jack, was with me. It's a trip that we will always remember. I love taking photos. My favorites are of elderly people, old country buildings, and my Border collies, Manna and Blaze.

PARIS-SANDLER, LAURA
I have always loved the awesomeness of the beaches and sunsets. When I see photos such as these, I feel drawn to the serenity and can just imagine the crashes of the waves while walking along the shores. To me, there is nothing like the peacefulness of a sun setting on the waters when the rays seem to echo all around their warmth and the closing of another day.

PATTERSON, RANDI
This is a picture of Peter Tork of the Monkees, which I took during one of their Anniversary Tours. The title is actually the closing theme for the TV show's second season. Growing up with the TV show, Peter was always my favorite Monkee. I had the opportunity to see Peter play his own music at a music store that has small intimate shows with singers and songwriters. I finally got to talk to Peter myself, one-on-one with no crowds, it was wonderful! Now my goal is to see his blues band!

PATTERSON, RICHARD
Living near the coast, I take a lot of beach photos. One Saturday last February, my wife and I had about ten feet of snow on the slopes above Lake Tahoe. I had a new camera I was itching to try out, and the weekend was ours. So we loaded the Jeep and headed into the mountains. Sunday afternoon we decided to head home with a few rolls of exposed film. Driving back is when I saw this peak along the ridge. I ran off eight or ten shots, but I knew instantly that this particular frame was the keeper.

PEARL, KATRINA
I took this photo of my son, Daniel, on Mother's Day 2004 when he was eight months old. I spent the whole afternoon taking pictures of Daniel and my daughter, Chelsea. I have been taking pictures since Chelsea was born almost eleven years ago. I just started entering my pictures in contests last year and have won several ribbons. It is a great pleasure to be chosen for your publication.

PETERSON, MARGARET
Our twins have been a great and fun blessing to us since they were born in May 2004. Each day has been an exciting experience as we watch Rex Jr. and Teah grow and explore so many things together. So you could imagine how excited we were that this picture came out so well and now the opportunity to share this moment of discovery with many others is such a joy. To see them play

together and be so happy is the best thing we could ever have hoped for!

PETERSON, REBECCA L.
The cat's name is Taz Angel, but she likes to be called Tazzie. She is one of several talented cats who share my home. (Some play pat-a-cake with me, two sisters give me eskimo kisses upon request. One meows when turned on her back, like a baby doll crying, and gives me "five." A few more jump into my arms.) Tazzie is an imp. She hated the name Taz, so one day while I was holding her I told her "Taz is one of my favorite cartoon characters. What do you want me to call you, anyway, angel?" Tazzie looked at me and winked. There really isn't a human baby in the house. I bought the pacifiers for my niece to play with the baby dolls. Tazzie liked to chew on them and carry them around, so I grabbed a camera and caught the moment. There is a camera in my car, and one in nearly every room of my house. One never knows when a great picture will just beg to be captured!

PETRAUSKAS, RUTH
I immigrated to the United States from Germany in 1950. I was a bookkeeper, and later got a degree in Accounting. My love for Shepherd was from early love of my parent's dog and watching our city's police dog training on Sunday mornings. Apollo, featured in this photograph, was different. As a young puppy, he was an ugly duckling with hanging ears and knobby knees. I picked him because of his fathomless eyes, which drew me to him in an unexplainable way. He proved to be outstanding in his obedience performances and behavior in public forums. Thirteen years after his death, he had the honor of his photo winning the International Library of Photography Contest. The ugly duckling has become a beautiful swan.

PETRZEL, ALOIS J.
I took my first picture, "NDC," in the Czech Republic in the village Buchlovice, where this chateau and castle is located. I was visiting my brothers, sister, and friends. I was born not too far in the city UH Hraniste, South Moravia. I took my other picture, "Beach Day, Cape Cod," while vacationing on Cape Cod. Cape Cod is wonderful in all four seasons.

PHAM, TERRI
This is my best friend, James, sitting on top of one of the temples in Chichen Itza overlooking the world. I love this photo because it captures his pure essence. Chichen Itza was the first of many adventures that we shared together.

PHELPS, KAREN
My granddaughter loves to ride horses and ponies. Since she lives in a place too small for a real pony, she usually rode a rocking horse. This day she found a pet as big as a pony. I took this picture because she looks like she is explaining that he is going to be a pony and she is the rider and he seems to be listening carefully to her every word.

PHILLIPS, KAREN L.
A distinguishing physical feature of the bichon frise breed of dog is their full beard and mous-

tache. As my dog, Buddy, and I walk through the neighborhood or park, my pet's natural, friendly charm toward people, other dogs, and children is phenomenal. I'm most grateful to him for many reasons, not the least of which is that he has brought experiences and other people into my life that, normally, I would not have had a chance to share, meet or know. And, of course, all owners of dogs (or pets) share a bond as real as people and their children.

PHILLIPS, DAVID A., II
The photograph of this angel is a wonderful way that I remember one of my closest neighbors. I chose this name, because Margie was a special person in my life. I grew up with her as my neighbor, teacher, and friend. She was an accomplished pianist and musician. Every morning, I would awaken to her playing the piano. I took piano from her for three years. When I was twelve, she developed a brain tumor and died. I stopped playing the piano, because it made me think of Margie Brown. That's why this photograph is called "Margie's Angel."

PILLER, LISA
Photography has always been a passion of mine. I just love taking pictures of everything. I have just recently decided to make photography my profession. This photograph was taken on my first trip to Las Vegas. At night I would go outside on the strip and I was in such awe. All the lights were so beautiful and amazing. Someday I hope to travel and photograph all the wonders of the world.

PIZZARDI, FRANK S.
I have been doing photography for ten years. My work includes flowers, landscapes, memorabilia and old buildings. My work has received first place and an honorable mention from Cape Fear Camera Club and Slow County Arts Council. The Jacksonville daily news featured an article on my most recent work. In the past four years, my focus has been old buildings and the history they represent. My vision is for you to have the experience of imagining the people and events that gave these buildings life.

PLASTER, JAMIE
Since our daughter has come into our lives, we have been capturing many special moments. This photo was taken on her birthday when she was two months old. Jalen Michael and I were playing on the floor and I took this photo of us. It is a family favorite.

PONTIVEROS, BENNY
I am from Majayjay, Laguna, Philippines. I grew up in the farm from a family of five. I have a Mining Engineer degree from Manila, Philippines. I worked in copper, gold, silver mines in Philippines. With our six kids and my wife, Lucy, I migrated to St. Albans, West Virginia in 1982. My wife and I worked for the State Department of Environmental Protection. My hobbies are hunting, fishing, mountain bike riding, and nature photography. Honesty is always my best policy in life. We visited my hometown last January/February and went for a picnic to the Taytay Waterfalls.

PORTSMOUTH, BOB
When I retired in 2001, I received my first digital camera as a retirement gift from my wife. I spent many hours learning different settings and shots. On our first camping trip in the spring, I shot this picture against what I witnessed to be a beautiful sunset. I thought the colors to be incredible. The silhouette of the trees along the banks of the Sheep River in Alberta against this remarkable sunset created this picture I proudly named "Evening Shades."

POSTMA, ROBERT SHANE
On the night of November 7, 2004, a friend alerted me that the sky had turned a wonderful colour. Indeed it had as you can see in this photo. Photographing the Northern Lights has always interested me. Take some time and enjoy. I work as a nurse practitioner in the Yukon Territory in Northern Canada.

POWELL, NICOLE
This is a photo of my seven-year-old son, Nicholas. He was a premature baby who has many special needs, one of which is autism. I'm a stay-at-home mom who has been quite busy since Nicholas was born. This day in particular, Nicholas wanted to get up in that tree and pretend he was a monkey. I thought that was funny because I have always called him my little monkey since birth, because he was born three months premature and actually looked like a little red monkey. He loves to climb everything and in this picture he looked like he was an angel, my angel.

POWELL, WANDA
This is my son, Mardy, telling his nephew, Dayne, about one of God's beautiful creations, the bluebirds. My family shares many happy times outdoors. This photo was taken on such a day!

POWERS, BETH
This is a photo of my niece, Leslie, and her son, Jacob. I am an avid picture taker and always have my camera. This was not a planned shot, it just happened! Jacob was just giving his mommy kisses and as you can see, he loves his mommy! There is nothing more powerful than a mother and her child. This picture will make a lasting memory.

PRATT, TRENA
This photo was taken in a field on our farm in South Point, Ohio. The little girls the picture are my daughters, Hannah, age six, and Haylee, age three. My husband, Ed, and I operate a greenhouse business at our home and milk dairy cattle with his family. I have always enjoyed thought-provoking photography and was pleasantly surprised when this photo turned out so well.

PRICE, JEREMY
My photo was taken in November 2002 and is of my children, Sally, age seven, and James, age five. The story behind it is their grandfather, Bill, had recently moved nearby and bought a new refrigerator. I salvaged the huge five-foot tall box and took it home for them to play in. Once they had crawled into the box, I opened it so there was no escape, but cut a window in it so they could peer out cheekily! I guess this picture really captured their playful spirit at the time, and the cardboard frame really enhances the effect.

PRICE, W. V.
At age ninety-five, I've been a photographer for eighty years. I cherish my amateur status and enjoy competition. This candid shot of my two-year-old was a prizewinner in 1948. On a family fishing outing, my son had an unexpected dip in the lake, so my wife dressed him in a makeshift shirt. Undeterred, my little boy came running to pick up the fishing pole and I picked up my camera. As a retired banker and POW survivor from World War II, I find satisfaction in recording portraits, everyday scenes, and still life arrangements.

PYLE, SHIRLEY MAY
One day while sitting on our front porch with my husband, Gary, I noticed that the hummingbirds would still come to the feeder nearby if we stayed very still. I decided to go a step further and see if they would still come if I held the feeder. As you can see, they were willing, as long as I did not move. I love to have creatures of nature as my subjects, whether I am using my camera or my paintbrush.

QUESADA, ELYSSA
This is a picture of my friend, Car. My favorite part of this picture is how the highlights in her hair vividly stand out in the brilliant morning sunlight. I also love how the leading lines of the bleachers correspond with her legs.

RAD, FANNI
A child is the most beautiful precious gift given by God, a miracle of life that inspires you to go beyond your limits to do wonderful things. Taking the picture of my baby is one of those wonderful things.

RAHNENFUEHRER, MARGE
This is a picture of my five-year-old granddaughter, Kaylee, and my timneh African gray parrot, Annie. Kaylee loves animals and wants them all to love her too. She wanted to hold Annie so bad, but when she actually had her on her arms, she wasn't quite so sure of that beak! It all ended happily when the photo was shot after this one showed a beautiful smile. Photography is a hobby of mine, and I try to keep a camera close at hand. I got lucky with this one.

RANDALL, LINDA
On a recent trip to Rajistan in western India, I took a brief camel safari into the Thar Desert to watch the sunset over the sand dunes. Our camel driver and his young son captivated my imagination. I was able to capture their beautiful and penetrating eyes in this photo and they continue to speak to me of the hard and simple lives of these desert people. I love having my pictures around me, they remind me of all the wonderful places I have visited and how lucky I am.

RAPUANO, SARA
"Solitary Blossom" is from a sunflower my mom saved in 1997 from her brother's funeral. Every summer she plants the seeds saved from one of the new blossoms. This year she planted over twenty-five seeds but the chipmunks ate all the

seedlings. Mom was afraid this would be the last year for saving these sentimental seeds. As you can see, this was the only sunflower that survived, with many seeds saved for this year's planting. I took this photo to remind her what she taught me about gardening. Planting a garden is believing in tomorrow!

REHBEIN, PAM

Our puppy, Gypsie Rose, has had a rough start to life. Your contest just hit me at Valentine's Day. Gypsie Rose was found with her sister, Sheba, in a box at a truck stop in Sacramento, California. My brother, Jim, is a trucker and his dog, Cassie, found the two puppies. I took one and so did Jim. Oh yeah, we're in good old Wisconsin! When Valentine's Day came, I took this picture and sent it to all our friends and family, especially Daddy. Daddy loved getting a picture of his little girl. Of course I'm taken!

REHM, KIM

Our house is close to where the Niagara River meets Lake Ontario, so we have spectacular views of Toronto. This particular day was very special. My family was gathered together for a day at the lake. It was the first time we had been together in a long time. My nieces, Ashley and Morgan, and nephews, Josh and Anthony, spent the entire day boating, picnicking, and walking on the beach. We had so much fun and this sunset was actually the perfect ending to a perfect day. My husband, Ed, and I still to this day reminisce about that beautiful summer day in July 2002.

REYNOLDS, ELLEN SCURRY

My friend loves irises and has them planted in her yard. I took this picture so that she could use it as her screensaver at work.

REYNOLDS, KOURTNI

Pictures can truly capture special memories that last a lifetime. This picture of the beautiful sunset I took at my aunt and uncle's lake is truly a sign from God. It reminds me how God is always with us and His creations are beautiful. I decided to take the picture of the sunset to remind me that God is always near. Every time I look at the picture I took, it reminds me that "God's Glory Shines."

RHODES, STACIE S.

I was at the local warm spring getting ready for my final day of my Scuba diving course. It was a beautiful morning that I wanted to capture forever. I love sunrises and sunsets, especially around water. Light and water are very captivating to me. I take my camera everywhere I go. My photos are glimpses into my life; they are like my journal.

RIESTER, WINNIE

Jasmine is my granddaughter's cat who lives with us and is unique in not only her markings but in the fact that she lives off the land for six months of the year. She has being doing this for the past five years. We live in upstate New York where winters get cold. Jazzy is a house cat until around May when she wants to go out. She hangs around for a week or so and then is gone until the snow flies. I love taking pictures, especially if the subject is unaware. Most of my

family tries to hide when they see me coming with my camera.

RIETA, RANIE

This is our daughter, Fiona. I have been documenting her baby activities since the day she was born: the first time she cracked a smile, the first time she nibbled her finger, the first time she successfully rolled over. More of these milestones have been captured on film as we watch her grow right before our eyes. My wife and I are always delighted every time we turn each page of our daughter's photo albums. I believe that these pictures will always be treasured, even many years from now, because they spark beautiful memories that are truly timeless.

ROBERTS, NANCY E.

This is a picture of my son, Al, at his last football game of the season. It was a losing season with one win all year. I could see and feel his need to win this game by all his actions the week before the game. It was a local rival game held annually every Thanksgiving Day. His facial expression shows his concentration, determination, passion, and his will to win the game. My love for photography, encouraged by my doctor and family, has healed me through my pictures. They bring me to a better place and a smile always comes to my face.

ROGERS, JERRI

I am the official photographer for my family. This is my daughter, who is one of my best models. This was an experiment in North Window Light technique. I am very proud of how well it showed my daughter's beauty and inner spirit.

ROGERS, JOE

I was with friends on an annual trip when Tyler and I jumped upon a rickety old wagon pulled by two huge horses that was touring the town of Red Lodge, Montana. Upon the last stop of our journey through town, I snapped five shots of the same situation not knowing how they would come out. I knew the men to the front would look great, but I didn't realize that a small child had taken interest in what I was doing. It wasn't until I developed the film that I noticed the child had looked right into the camera at one particular point. With one snap of the shutter, I had captured a great moment in time.

ROGERS, RAMONA

This is proof that the joys and awes of snow are never-ending for my little Florida girl, even after the sun goes down.

ROJAS, EM

Derby week in Louisville is a great place to be. The people, the horses, and the festivities are much more than the two-minute race. While dining downtown, I was enchanted by the bustle and carriages going to and fro. As you can see, more than racehorses are at work for the event. This dapple gray's meter had expired. I love taking snapshots of life. I often draw and paint from these snippets.

ROZBICKA, HELENA

This is a photo of my grandson held in an embrace

by his mother, my daughter. It is a personal and intimate moment, but also universal in showing the eternal bond of a simple extension of the hand of a baby towards his mother. The colors and lighting are reminiscent of Dutch paintings.

RUBLE, DEANNA

This photo is of my friend and her two-week-old little girl. My friend struggled with infertility for years and had many surgeries, which resulted with only thirty percent of one ovary. The doctor told her she only had a small percentage of getting pregnant in a certain amount of time. That time passed and then thinking she would never conceive, she did with no medical help! Her daughter is a true "Miracle From God." This photo is what motivated me to go into portrait photography, my dream since high school. I now have opened my own studio.

RUSHLOW, ELIZABETH

This photo is of my husband, Dave, who has been an avid surfer and beach and ocean lover all of his life. I took this picture of sunrise right in front of our beach house in Garden City, SC. I captured all the physical and emotional feelings that the beautiful sunrise and ocean have to offer. We both have spent many hours at the beach and love to watch the ocean's constant changes. The colors, sounds, and smells that we experience at the ocean give us peace and serenity from our everyday hectic lives.

SADOWSKI, KIMBERLY J.

This photo was taken in my hometown of Hartford, Wisconsin. I went to a small pond/fishing area we have there. I had an idea of the sort of pictures I wanted to take, but when photographing nature, you never know what you'll get. I am proud I was lucky enough to immortalize this one moment. I wanted this photo to remind people to relax and that simple moments make the best memories.

SAETERN, CHRISTY

This is my very first cat, Kitty. She came into my life as a stray begging for food. I've had her for over a year now and she has gotten rid of my sister's fear of cats. She now enjoys cats as much as I do. Kitty had inspired me with a lot of things and I'm glad she chose to beg at my door.

SAKA, CAMILLE

As a graphic artist, I'm more accustomed to creating graphics than taking photos, but I have always loved taking pictures of my children. Over the years, they have focused on milestones, such as birthdays and first steps. It's especially rare to capture on film a young child during a "quiet" moment. This photo was taken when my oldest daughter, Brenda, now almost thirteen, was two years old. It captures her thoughtfulness and maturity, even at such a young age. It reminds me of the depth of thought and feeling that toddlers can experience. Brenda continues to amaze me nine years later.

SALMO, TRACEY

It's a beautiful evening at a skate park. My daughter always wanted to capture that ball in the sky and this is as close as she can get, looking very proud with her friend visiting from Hawaii. Life is full of breathtaking moments. To capture those brief seconds is amazing but special.

SANDERS, EDWARD RICHARD
This is a picture of my friend. He swims with me and visits every afternoon. This afternoon it was rainy and the pine tree he is under serves as some protection.

SANDERSON, FRANCESCA
This is such a truly apt title. She grows in wisdom and grace. She is my youngest grandchild of nine. Her wistfulness captures the expectance of a wonderful future. I took this picture in her Easter bonnet while visiting her family. I am a picture taker rather than a photographer, but I know a special moment in time when I see one.

SCHERER, DAVID A.
My interest in photography began when I was a young man. My mother relinquished several books of the old merchandising trading stamps to purchase my first camera. I've always preferred candid and stopping the action types of photography. It's also advantageous to always have your camera handy. I was going to assist this chipmunk out of the bird feeder but it didn't need any help. It scampered up and out of the feeder all by itself through the narrow opening at the top.

SCHMIEDLIN, CHUCK
Autumn has always been my favorite time of the year. On this particular morning, Mocha and I were standing on the deck, when I noticed the sun's reflection was giving her a golden glow. I went inside to get my camera and was able to capture this photo, which I call "Mocha Gaze."

SCHRYVER, SHAI M.
This picture was taken in the car on my way home from Canada. My mother and I took a day trip and it was a long drive. I was looking out the window at the scenery when I decide that the northwest is a great place with a great view. That day I took about a hundred pictures, which I showed to my mom. She really liked them and so did a lot of other people. That's when I decided that it's nice to stop and take a look around once in a while.

SCHUETZ, SHIRLEY V.
This photo was taken during the Schuetz family Christmas, spent on the Oregon coast in December 1999. While walking on the beach on one of the few days without rain, I took this picture of the Yaquina Lighthouse, our scenic companion throughout our vacation, just as the sun was breaking through the clouds. As the lighthouse guides ships, the sun was guiding us to follow its rays.

SCHWAN, LAURIE
I took this photo of my oldest son in hopes of using it for his senior pictures. It was my first experiment with black and white. As a mother of four, I take several hundred pictures every year. I am now getting into the outdoor scenes, as my husband is an avid hunter. Everywhere I go I have my camera with me!

SCIPIO, TENEFER
This photo was taken my first year away at college. My love for photography was great and still growing, as I took my first college course in photography. The joy of having a camera and darkroom at my disposal was overwhelming. I chose the name, "Tourist," because in the photo I looked like I was a tourist and also because I had a crush on a guy who I thought was great and respected a lot. His name is Taurus. Unfortunately, because of financial situations, my freshman year was my last year at Oakwood College. Whenever I look at this photo, I think of my one great year away at school, all the friends I made, all the fun I had, and most of all, the memories I hold for that great school year in March 2004.

SEABURG, LINDSAY MARIE
This photo was taken at the Minnesota Zoo. I have always enjoyed going to the zoo and taking pictures of the animals. The dolphins have always been my favorite except they're a lot harder to capture since they move around so fast. With my last stop for the day, I had hoped to get a glimpse of the dolphins with my camera. I hadn't been in the room that long looking at dolphins through the glass. I was just hoping to get a close-up of these beautiful creatures. With my camera in my hand, all of a sudden I had the dolphin looking right at me. I was so surprised and happy just hoping that the shot would turn out. Needless to say, the photo did turn out. I couldn't have gotten a better picture that day at the zoo. I'm so very proud and happy to share my talent.

SEXTON, CARMEN A.
My husband, Gerald, and I just celebrated our forty-third anniversary. We have four grandchildren, Steven, seventeen, Javier, fifteen, Michael, five, and Alyssa, four. We live in a small community where families and friends get involved with the children, including church events, sports, family gatherings, etc. I have been a caregiver for my grandchildren. At one time, I quit my job to care for them during a family tragedy. I also worked to help pay for my husband's education. Now he's a retired teacher. I have made scrapbooks and photo albums for each one of my grandchildren. I enjoy them and every time I get a chance, my camera is ready to take pictures. I have also taught them love and respect. They are straight A students in school.

SHAFRON, MARILYN
I take a lot of pictures and am very interested in photography. We have a wall in our kitchen with about thirty 12"x18" prints displayed. We call this wall our happiness wall because we have these large pictures of our loved ones who have passed away, also of our three children at various ages, and our nine grandchildren. We also have great pictures taken around our area of Gates Mills during the seasons of the year. This picture of the owls and fruit, according to my family, is truly a magnificent photo and our friends and family love it. Good family pictures are a sure cure for depression.

SHERRY, MARIA
When I first traveled west, I was amazed at how different sunsets were there from the East Coast. My husband and I would often go searching for

the perfect place to view the next one. One search led to the University of Arizona, where a small hill boasts a giant "A" in homage to the school. That hill has been dubbed "A" Mountain by the students there, and it was from the topmost vantage point that I was able to capture the beauty of those desert sunsets, and the striking silhouette of my husband, who shared them all with me.

SIEGWART, JENNIFER
I am currently in my third year of study at Brooks Institute of Photography. Although it is a commercially driven school, my passion lies within fine art. This image was taken in my hometown, Palmdale, California. I feel that this image is a good depiction of life in a small town. Now that I am older, I have come to see past the desolation of such a place and focus on the beauty it holds. Places such as this are my favorite to photograph because of the stories that can be told through the image.

SIERRA, CHRISTINA
This is a picture of my daughter, Briana, who is my youngest of four daughters. Having three older teenage daughters, Christily, seventeen, Jesenia, fifteen, and Karla, thirteen, when Briana came along, I was out of practice in the potty training department. This picture of Briana exemplifies her shared confusion during potty training. Briana is not your average baby. She is extremely bright and strong-willed like all the women in her life including her grandma Janie and her auntie Sonia, who she absolutely adores. She looks just like her daddy, Marlo, who is absolutely crazy about her.

SINQUEFIELD, JERRY
The Bent Walnut tree is at the entrance to my brother and sister-in-law's, from and for which the entrance road is named. When the farm was first acquired, our neighbor brought us a picture of the Bent Walnut against a beautiful sunset. Because of the unique character of the tree, it is very eye-catching.

SIPES, ROD
My love for photography and nature led me to take this photograph while I was walking around Sea World with my granddaughter, Raquel. I never leave home without my camera and when I saw this beautiful flower, she was begging me to take her picture. There is nothing more spectacular than Mother Nature in a photograph.

SMALL, CAROLE
This photograph is of Andrew Golino and Alexis Rider taken at the wedding of Andrew's dad and Alexis's mom, Mr. and Mrs. John Golino Jr. on June 12, 2004 at Sedgely's in Greene, Maine.

SMART, APRYLE B.
A picture to me is like a memory forever captured on film. When you look at a picture, the first thing you remember is where you were when that picture was taken. This was my first time in New York; I think I took a picture of everything I saw. This picture holds a special memory for me, seeing the Twin Towers for the first time, not knowing eleven months later they would be forever changed.

My thoughts and prayers go out to everyone affected by 9/11.

SMITH, BARBARA

My sister, Jackie, and I decided to revisit our birth state of Georgia and while touring the small town of Madison, we were transfixed at the wayside flower garden. The pink beauty of these hollyhocks seems to be ringing in the glory of summer.

SMITH, DANIEL A.

I live in beautiful Sunriver, Oregon. I graduated from the University of California in Berkeley in 1951. I am a retired Aerospace Engineer and I'm now an active fisherman and golfer. My main hobby is photography. In August of 2004, I was taking pictures of our flower garden. The honeybees were very active that day and as I snapped a close-up picture of a Gaillardia flower, a honeybee suddenly landed in the center of the flower. The entire event occurred so fast and was so amazing, that I sent the great picture in for your photo contest. I entitled the picture "Busy Bee."

SMITH, JENNIFER

This photograph was taken at Henricus Park, the site of an early English settlement on the James River. It was a sunny day in late summer. I was casually shooting pictures from an overlook when I noticed the old remains of a pier down below along the riverbank. I cautiously made my way close enough to snap a few photos right after a barge crossed the horizon creating the slight ripples in the water. I am an art major at John Tyler Community College, working towards transferring to VCU as a photography major.

SMITH, JOYCE ANN

This is my first granddaughter. Her name is Morgan Tayor. She loves the camera. Every time she would see me, she would say, "Take my picture, Granny. She is three years old. She is my little angel and I love her so much.

SMITH, JUDY R.

This "trout" was "caught" in Red River, New Mexico, after a Fourth of July parade. Afterwards, we were on our way to fish. My husband, Randall, who was driving, suddenly pulled off the road. Motioning to me to follow, he handed me the camera to me. "Stay right there!" he commanded. Picking up his fishing rod, he said, "OK. Take a picture." The real artistry belonged to the group of citizens who built the trout on a frontloader. This was the biggest fish caught that day or any day!

SMITH, NATHAN

When I took this photo, I was searching for the unusual while walking through an outdoor sculpture museum in St. Louis. I captured a small section of the original, which was made of rusted metal, small bird cages, and broken glass. To me, it resembled a village, or perhaps city apartment buildings. Once the pride of the community, it is now a forgotten relic. I was trained in studio fine art, which brought to this photograph an artistic creativity. This, blended with the classic aspects of black and white photography, helps create such artistic visions as my "Sculpted Village."

SORENSEN, JENNIFER

Jennifer Sorensen, fifty, of Fairmont, Minnesota, has an interest in local photography of an agricultural community in southern Minnesota's Prairie Pothole region. Jennifer works both in the fields of special education and nursing. Her two children are in college. Her husband, John, is employed in the field of computer/electronic design engineering. Her photos have recently been displayed in a regional art fair/fundraiser, and are used in advertising and featured in a Christmas card.

SPADONI, BRANDON RONALD

I was surprised one day when I went over to my grandparents' house to hear a clicking sound at the edge of their long driveway. Looking down, I discovered a baby owl on the ground that had fallen through its nest. My granddad and I repaired the nest and put the baby owl back inside with its sibling. I enjoyed taking pictures and watching the owls thrive under the care of their mother until they were able to fly away. This is only one of the many photos I took. It was the highlight of my summer.

SPEIRS, GORDON L.

My wife and I decided to go visit Japan, since my son's wife is from Japan. We stayed at my son's in-laws' home. They showed us around Japan. I like to take pictures of places where we have visited. It just happened that I was at the right place and time when I took this picture.

STARR, DEBORAH LYNN

One evening, my son and I were visiting a park by the Ohio River. I always have a camera close by and could not resist this beautiful sunset. The serenity and peacefulness of this photo made it a favorite for my family and me. When I gaze at this photo, I am reminded that God's creation is indeed beautiful and unique.

STEBNER, THERESA

While vacationing in the Hamptons on Long Island, my six-year-old son, Christopher, marveled at how beautiful the sky looked. It was the perfect picture to end our unforgettable two-week vacation. The image of the sky that night will stay with us, along with our wonderful memories of that 2004 summer vacation.

STEFFY, STELLA M.

Our tiger-striped cat was a stray we took into our home. A most loving and friendly cat, he roamed the house at night and slept most of the day, except when he heard the birds chattering outside the kitchen window. We lost him a few months ago, and I still miss him. He was sixteen years old. If there's a kitty heaven, he's there! His final resting place will have flowers always!

STEPHENSON, RICHEL LESLIE

This is photo of my son, Kaden. He is twelve weeks old in this picture. We were getting him ready for his baptism. I propped him up on his teddy bear and snapped the photo before he slid over. This photo is just priceless to me, and I have a lot of pictures of Kaden. Thank you for seeing how special this shot is. Kaden is the true artist.

STEVENS, ANDREW E.

"The Feast" is one of a group of photographs I took about fifteen years ago on my visit to Kenya. It was early morning at daybreak. When the animals of the jungle started stirring, the zebras were the first in multitude of numbers. They were running, as other wild animals chased them. It did not take long before the female lions observed the stampede of the zebras. They picked their victims and it wasn't difficult! My lion started slowly, but accelerated to the speed of the zebra's, caught her in that fast movement, jumping on her, penetrating her sharp teeth into the poor zebra's jugular vein, pulled her down to the ground, and dragged her to the shade. By that time, the members of the lion's family gathered and "The Feast" began.

STONE, DONNA M.

I'm a mother of three children, three dogs, and a cat; they keep me busy. I do find the chance to snap a picture or two like this of our Lab. I like to catch them off guard; those are the best photos I think. My husband, Rick, leaves the picture taking to me as he says I have an eye for it. I'm not sure, but I loved this shot.

STOUT, LOUIS

While on a photography trip through the western part of the United States in 2004, "The Beauty Of Nature At Jackson Hole" was created in Jackson Hole, Wyoming. This picture was taken in the early morning and I feel the title speaks for itself, for there is nothing more beautiful than nature. The Teton Mountain region is the most exciting place that I have visited that offers great outdoor picture making. I visualized this shot for an hour and half before it became a reality. Thanks for the opportunity to be a part of your program.

STUMP, SHANNON

I have always enjoyed taking pictures. I take my camera almost everywhere I go. My favorite subjects to photograph are family, family pets, and nature. This photo is my sister, Sarah, and her colt, Charmer. While training in the arena, they both stopped to look at another one of our horses and that's when I snapped the picture. Their look and the expressions were great! My sister and I have been involved with horses since we were in elementary school. They taught us discipline and responsibility. I love taking pictures and wish to pursue it on a professional level.

STUMPF, JOSEPH A., III

"City's Peace" is twilight, the magical inner landscape of Minneapolis, Minnesota. The light in the picture is an invigorating example of the joy of photography and activity that anyone can experience. This is how I see the beauty in just about everything. It shows the beauty of new architecture, warmth of walkways, and peace one can enjoy even in the city at night. In my photography is a joy I share to inspire you, to feel what you see, and be one in peace.

SZYMANSKI, DONALD C.

I had gone down to Orlando, Florida for a visit to Disney World. I took this hot air balloon ride on the morning of April 7, 2004 with Orange Blossom Balloons. This was my third trip on a hot air balloon. We had to stay up in the air for an hour and then came down slowly back on the ground. I have been retired for three years. I have lived in Laurence Harbor, New Jersey for fifty-six years. My hobbies are digital photography, travel, my cat, and the fish tank.

TAMBURELLO, ROBERT

This photo was taken with an Olympus C8080 digital camera at f8 50150 on October 7, 2004. My wife and I were on our twenty-fifth anniversary cruise. We came across this gentleman on the island of Mykonos, Greece. He sat peacefully with a small tissue in his hand waiting for someone. This is one of my favorites taken on this trip. This trip was a photographer's dream. Everyone should carry a camera with him or her wherever they go. You never know when you will be able to frame a memory.

TEETERS, PAT BILBY

Montana is the love of my life. My mom grew up on a ranch in central Montana, where I've visited many summers. One day my husband, Darrel, and I were walking on my Uncle Bill Hassler's ranch near Hilger when we discovered this photograph waiting to be taken. It exemplifies all that I love about Montana, especially the "Big Sky." I am a newspaper owner, writer and editor for our family's senior newspaper, The Valley Messenger, in Yucaipa, California. Photography and oil painting are my favorite hobbies.

TERLITZ, SUZANNE NEWMAN

As a Speech Pathologist working with preschool disabled children, I find taking photographs great stress relief. I put the pictures up all around my office. I enjoy taking photographs of many different subjects. Springtime brings many flowers, blossoms, and insects to my yard. One day, I caught two swallowtails flying around the yard, one looking for food, one looking for a mate. I followed them around the yard like a crazy person hoping to catch them in one frame. After many attempts, I captured their images and "Courtship In Flight" was the end result, of which I am very proud!

THAYNE, EDWARD D.

I am Edward D. Thayne, age fifty-seven. I was working a sincerity job and one off the workers said that there was a robin's nest in a bush. I took a number of pictures from the eggs until they left the nest. I take pictures all the time of just about anything. From sunsets to pets, nothing is off limits. I've sent pictures into The International Library of Photography since 1998. My wife helps pick the pictures and titles.

THOMPSON, HUNTER OWEN

Hunter took this photo while on a class trip in eighth grade to Oxaca, Mexico. He is an avid photographer and possesses an eye for capturing people and places with great feeling and composition.

THOMPSON, LORI

I'm a registered nurse with a love for photography. I love to capture memories on camera, memories my family can share over and over again. This photo captures one of those times you want to cherish forever. We laugh each time we look at this picture. Our precious little ones are only little for a while. So we need to enjoy and cherish that very little time we get with them, because we can't go back in time and do it again. This little sleeping beauty is the love of my life and that will never change!

THORNTON, LINDA

I am a fifty-six-year-old female in a little country town called Coldsprings, Texas. It's a very quiet little fishing town with a lot of good things to take pictures of. I've always loved taking pictures. My grandchildren tore up my yard getting this puppy out of a sewer line. She was a good dog. Her color always fascinated me; she blended with the colors of the woods. The dog's name was Tiny. We don't have her anymore, but she was an inspiration to my grandchildren and me. I live with my life partner, who's twenty-three years old. My grandchildren are all teenagers now, but they still visit. But now, I have my new great-grand baby to take pictures of. Her name is Breetinna Marie Thornton.

TRAVIS, RODNEY H.

We took a trip over a mountain pass this past winter. When we drove along a cliff area on Hwy 12, the fog lying in the valley caught my eye. So I pulled over, got out, and took a series of three shots. "Valley Fog" was the most intriguing.

TREIBER, ALBERT DAVID

I took this picture while on an extended deployment in the Persian Gulf in support of Operation Iraqi Freedom. The ship I am on normally operates anywhere from four hours of flight quarters to eighteen hours a day/night depending on our schedule, which changes at a moment's notice. I am a big fan of sunsets; they are my favorite kind of picture to take. Sunsets set the mood for the day to come. I relax in the warmth they provide as they are setting back into the horizon. I think about the day's events and about when we turn around and head for home. Persian Gulf sunsets are the best because they continuously change from the time they start to set (orange skies) to when they are gone, turning the skies a mixture of colors, only to be repeated the following day and night.

TROUTMAN, SAM, JR.

This is my son, Steve, who at the time of this photograph was in his mid-thirties and still racing. The photo was taken at a motocross track in Steele, Alabama and is one of those priceless one in a million shots.

TULLIS, PATRICIA R.

I'm an older person, but I feel like I'm seventeen years old again. My husband died in 2000, which is also when my new husband's wife died. We met on a blind date where my cousin introduced us. We were on a family trip to Oregon and our second honeymoon and drove along the coastline, which is just beautiful.

ULATOUSKI, MARGARET

They say a picture is worth a thousand words, however, only one photo does not tell the whole story of the frogs. Every night, they come to my parents' home in Fort Lauderdale, Florida because they love my dad's cooking, especially his spaghetti, as you can see by the smile on their faces! I live in Philadelphia, but my dad cares for them in my absence. When I visit, they actually come out to greet me. I specialize in photographing people, special events, parties and celebrities as well as web site design and photos.

VALDEZ, CRYSTAL

This is my precious daughter, Jendaya. We had just moved to Germany with the military. I wanted her to have wonderful memories of her childhood so I took this picture in our German city named Gelnhausen. Jendaya had just recently learned to stand up. I couldn't resist snapping shot after shot. Jendaya, you are the joy of my life, and you make me laugh and smile every day. I couldn't imagine my life without you. You are everything wonderful, baby girl. May the Lord of peace Himself give you peace at all times and in every way. I love you.

VALERO, JILL

One of the simple pleasures in life that I truly enjoy is spending my summer days on the beach. My fiancé, Earl, took my dog, Clyde, and me to Santa Cruz for the first time. The title came from one of my favorite movies, "A Walk to Remember." The picture clearly shows Earl and Clyde enjoying their view on the beach. Each time I look at this picture, I remember everything that day, from the touch of the sand, the smell of the sea, the feel of the wind, the sound of the waves, and the view of my two loved ones on the beach. It was my last exposure on my film and I saw both Earl and Clyde looking at the waves. I waited for the waves to crash and then I took my last picture. It's a view I'll always remember.

VAN WIJK, HELENA GIJSBERS

I was born and grew up in Czechoslovakia, a small country in the heart of Europe. When I first came to the United States, I was fascinated by the American melting pot, the nation composed of people of all kinds of nationalities, ethnic origins, social and economical backgrounds, religions, customs, and skin colors. The picture was taken in Houston, Texas, at the Westheimer Street Festival, an annual event that brings together people from all walks of life. I believe that this picture perfectly illustrates the diversity of this nation. I currently reside in Pasadena, Texas, with husband, Peter, and daughter, Amy.

VANDERHOEF, DEBBIE

Living in southeast Texas, we rarely see snow. The last time it snowed here was December 1988. So, when it snowed on Christmas Eve 2005, my entire family was shocked, including our four-year-old pit bull, Ziggy. She loved chasing the snowflakes, and we loved watching her. Ziggy is patiently waiting for her next big snow!

VARGO, SAMANTHA

I have many albums full of pictures of friends, strangers, family and everything else you can think of. My favorite pictures are of my daughters. This picture is of my oldest daughter, Megan. We were all in the backyard raking leaves. My grandmother commented on what a great picture this one turned out to be, and so here it is. I wish my other daughter, Jacklyn, would have been in it, but that's okay, maybe next time.

VARJU, JIMMIE
My memories were taking pictures as a child with my father. Just as he loved photography, he passed this love down to me. This photo was taken at Cranberry Glades in West Virginia as my family was on vacation, camping at Watoga State Park. We were on a hike through the botanical area and enjoying the scenery of this beautiful state when I spotted this butterfly taking an afternoon rest. It was a one shot moment. Just as I took the picture, it flew away.

VAUGHN, CHARLENE
My photo was taken just outside of Omaha at Wildlife Safari Park. It was taken near the visitor center there in a garden of flowers that particularly draws butterflies. My photo was taken while sitting on the ground amongst the flowers. It was about a thirty-minute wait for the right shot. Aside from my grandchildren, there is nothing more rewarding than a photo you took that just turned out great. As are grandchildren, butterflies are fast moving targets. This is a moment forever frozen in time.

VAYETTE, PAM
My love of nature has always been a consuming factor in my photo adventures. The natural beauty of the world is so wonderful. I took this photo at a local park in Lake Charles. It amazed me that the turtle, a very vulnerable animal, was so relaxed by his adversary.

VER WEY, GLENN
While watching my three-year-old granddaughter playing and thinking back to the days of old, I got to see how simple life was as a kid. I thought how nice it was to not have a worry in the world, just stepping on her reflection and soaking up the sun. Photography is my hobby and my photos leave you thinking, I hope.

VISO, NAOMI
My husband and I love the sport of hockey and are season ticket holders for our local American Hockey League team, the Chicago Wolves. I am usually wired in my seat for each game as I listen to the play by play on the radio while watching the action and taking photos. This picture was taken during the playoffs in 2004.

VOCCOLA, MICHELE
Every animal should be able to enjoy life. Every pet should be cherished. Not every canine has casual fashion sense and knows how to sport her shades.

VOLTURO, DENISE
All my life I've dreamt of expressing myself creatively. My true inspiration came with the birth of my children. I took this photograph of my two-year-old twin boys, Jared and Zachary, after instructing them to "give a brother kiss." My boys, now three-and-a-half, have a beautiful baby sister, Alexsandra. My wonderful husband, Mike, and I live to find things to do to make them smile. I am so in love, I could cry every time I look at them. I love writing about and photographing my

family. Thank you for letting me share the best part of my life.

WAGONER, PATSY
I own a small country store at Drake, Kentucky, outside of Bowling Green, Kentucky, where everyone in the community is like family. We're across from White's Chapel Church, where the photo was taken. We were all sitting together eating supper one stormy afternoon in November 2003. After the storm, the sun came out so bright. Someone called to us to come look at the double rainbow. I went to my car, got my camera, and took the photo. It wasn't until after I printed it that I realized the end of the rainbow went into the steeple of the church. Everyone loved the photo and helped me name it and also wanted me to enter it into the contest. So here it is. Everyone is so excited.

WALKER, RUTHA S.
My name is Rutha S. Walker. I live in the beautiful northwest. We are a family with several generations involved in the timber industry. The "My Little Logger" photo is of my son, Lee, and his son, Zach. Zach is very special, he is smart and outgoing, but he is special another way. Zach has a kidney transplant. Zach became ill with E coli poisoning at age two, lost both kidneys, then received his transplant from his maternal grandfather a year later. Zach is now living a normal life we are so grateful.

WALTER, DEBBIE L.
I took this picture on my way to work one morning. The dew reflecting on the grass and the beautiful sunrays made me pull over and snap this picture. Since this picture was taken, my soul mate and husband, Miles, of twenty years, died unexpectedly. My heart is broken, but when I look at this picture it makes me think of him and how beautiful his view from Heaven must be. I consider this picture my little piece of Heaven.

WARREN, JOAN
Sugar and Spice were two remaining kittens of a litter of six. They were abandoned at our new golf course when construction prevented their mother from returning to them. My husband and I took them home and they have been inseparable ever since. I enjoy taking pictures of them and also have a love of sunsets. Sugar and Spice have been featured in two different "Page-a-Day" cat calendars. Smokey, my older cat, was also featured in a daily desk cat calendar.

WATKINS, TERRI L.
This photo and its publication will be a lasting tribute to our beloved cat, Talker, who unfortunately was hit by a car on Labor Day in 1999. We all miss him a lot. He was so full of curiosity and personality, I couldn't pass up the opportunity when he was in the neighbor's yard poking his head through the hole as far as it would go, probably looking for greener catnip.

WAY, KATHRYN A.
This is a photo of Matthew, truly "Tellin' It Like It Is" to his long-suffering brother, Daniel, on a sleepy afternoon at home. To think, all he wanted to do was take a nap! I have enjoyed taking pic-

tures since childhood, when my father gave me a Brownie Instamatic camera for my eighth birthday. My favorite photographic subjects are animals (especially my pets) and people (especially my nieces and nephew). For me, taking a picture is the process of becoming part of the photograph. Capturing a special moment, to be enjoyed again and again, is truly a gift that I enjoy sharing with family and friends.

WEBSTER, B. JAMES
It was an early fall morning and it had rained the night before when I drove through the town of Shiprock, New Mexico on the old Highway 666 going south. Approximately ten miles out, I turned off on Navajo Route 13 that goes near the pinnacle. I think the pinnacle is one of the magnificent landmarks in our four corners' region. I grew up in three different Indian Boarding Schools; I met Stella, my bride of forty-one years, in the last one. We are both retired and we travel to different bowling, archery, and Senior Olympics events as competitors. Photography has always been my favorite hobby. Now that our sons have children, I can start my photography all over again with our grandson.

WEESNER, LORAH LYNNE
I was sitting in the living room with my oldest son, Evan. We were looking out the window watching the butterflies. I thought it was a great shot. I told Evan to watch from the window. We had three lovely butterflies flying from flower to flower. I took a few shots and went back inside to enjoy the peace of watching them with Evan.

WELLS-YOUNG, CARRIE
This is my sister, Kim. We were having sisterly chat on a Sunday afternoon, and I noticed the photo opportunity that lay before me. So I snapped my camera and this is what I got. I believe the golden hue really captures who she is without even having to meet her. It is said that a photograph takes a little piece of your soul. I feel that all my photos have a little soul in them.

WEST, OLIVIA
This is just one of those adorable Kodak moments I captured on film of my beautiful daughter, Victoria. She was six months old here when she tried to get out of her high chair for the first time and gave us this goofy pose right before she was about to eat. Victoria is two years old now and she never hesitates to show her unique personality and hilarious sense of humor to everyone around her, especially when they have a camera ready to capture her on film.

WHEELER, MELISSA
I took this picture of my son, Garrett, during the dog days of summer. It brought back memories of my dad and granddad out checking their crops. They would say, "Could Use A Little Rain."

WHISENHUNT, DONALD
Pawnee Count, Oklahoma holds an annual Oklahoma Gas and Steam Engine show. Entries to this event come from all over the United States. While attending this weekend event, I came upon this case steam engine tractor blowing its whistle at noon along with the other entries. These old

tractors from the good old days reminded me of my grandfather.

WHITAKER, LORI
This is a photo of my son, Brett. He was leaping and playing around in the ocean waves, and I kept taking pictures. I knew I got one of him falling, but didn't know until the film was developed that I caught this moment. I received a very good camera for Christmas a few years ago, for the purpose of taking originals to point. Once I started taking photos, I fell in love with photography. I am now enrolled at our community college to begin their Photography Technology course.

WHITE, KAREN
Searching high and low for food must have tired this furry feline out. Once he had a full belly, he decided to rest atop the woodpile at our friends' campsite. He woke up seconds before the picture, just after a long, peaceful nap in the sun! What great dreams he must have had!

WHITE, RICHARD L.
My wife, Jan, and I, both missionaries, were required to exit Mozambique to renew visas, so we visited Tanzania. I shot this while en route to Ngorongoro. The Massai of this area go to extremes to avoid being photographed, so I learned to take photos from the side window of the Land Rover while looking disinterestedly in another direction. I've been an amateur photographer for many years, but didn't expect decent photos under such circumstances, so we see a real blessing. We hope you enjoy it as well. Love to Paul and Jenni, who encouraged me to submit this photo.

WHITEAKER, CASEY
My family is my life and my pets are part of that. This is Crook, the first of my loves in my life. He finds peace in himself and all of his surroundings. No matter when, where, or how, he is always comfortable. He is my inspiration when it comes to my own peace and quiet, my serenity.

WHITT, PATRICIA
For me, getting a chance to shoot a photo like this doesn't come along very often. First, I'm not usually a morning person and also, when facing the sun, you are never sure how your photos will turn out. I love experimenting with photography and trying to find unique, unusual, and interesting subjects/scenes. I'm a down-home, small town person who enjoys whatever life has to offer.

WILEY, MITCHELL ARTHUR
When traveling to Key West, Florida, there is one sight a traveler mustn't miss and that is the sunset celebration, which is held at Mallory Square every evening. I attended this festival back in August of 2003 while vacationing in the Florida Keys. It's basically a sidewalk carnival complete with food and drink vendors, arts and crafts of all kinds, and street performers galore. This bagpipe player is only one of many. I know he's wearing a kilt, but to me, it looks like he's wearing a skirt. I guess he's trying to get in touch with his inner woman. This is Key West after all. This is but one of many photographs I took that day.

WILLIAMS, SARAH
In eighth grade, I had surgery. I was told my life had to change. No longer could I "play" as I had. Walking hurt, everything hurt. I thought my life went from color to black and white. My sister, Heather, said my perspective had to change and got me into photography. I now know that everything is about perspective. Black and white is beautiful with its shades and contrasts, as beautiful as color, as beautiful as my life. For me, the windmill illustrates the endless circle of life and the mailboxes, life's daily comings and goings.

WILSON, CARMEN ESTELLE
My name is Carmen Wilson. I am twenty-six years old and I live in Gadsden, Alabama. This is a picture of the two people I hold closest to my heart, my children. William Tahj Alexander Jones is seven years old and Cayden Phyllece Jones is two years old. At the time of this picture, Cayden was only a few months old. Her brother, William, was fascinated with her. He leaned over to play with her and she grabbed his face. You could just see the love in their eyes as they gazed at each other. I could not let that moment just slip away. They say a picture can say a thousand words. I feel this one speaks volumes.

WINANS, SCOTT
This portrait, "A Friend Loves At All Times," was taken on a beach in Alabama while our families were on vacation. We had decided that we would go take some photos on the beach of our families when this took place. Life can be an endless journey as these two remarkable children have shown us. They have taught us that love is truly unconditional and that friendship cannot be taken lightly. Matthew and Morgan are one month apart in age; they are like brother and sister in many ways. This photo has become an heirloom in our home, as the love of these two children has been a blessing to our families.

WITTMAYER, NORMA
All my life I have loved Montana, its pioneers, and history. This photograph portrays the 1906 Gold Coin Mill on a hillside and slabs for mine car tracks (minus rails) on stilts heading into the mill. Now picture small ore cars clanking through the door to drop their load for processing. Now listen! You can hear the noisy five stamp battery crushing pay dirt and miners anticipating how they are going to spend their gold found at grass roots. This is my inheritance and I touch its beauty and history daily. Thank you for appreciating what the Lord has given me to enjoy.

WOLLASTON, DOUGLAS E.
My wife, Debbie, and I live at the top of a hill, within the city limits of Morgan Hill, California. Because of our location, we are very open to the elements of the weather, and the ever-changing cloud formations. The visual impact of sunrises and sunsets has trained us to keep the camera close at hand. Here, I share with you, the intensity of one day's beginning, with "Sunrise In Morgan Hill."

WOOD, AUSTIN
It was a beautiful fall day. The leaves had turned colors. My family and I went for a picnic. It was a grand day and a beautiful memory caught on film. I love my son so. I will cherish that day and this photo forever.

WOOD, TERRY
Our home is nestled in the Blue Ridge Mountains. I keep my camera in my car, which allows me to capture wonderful pictures of God's beautiful creation. This was a family of geese out walking on a warm Sunday afternoon. There was dad, mom, and two babies. The father goose ran back and forth across the road, thus allowing his family a chance to escape. When I snapped the picture, it appeared as if he was being left behind.

WOOD, THOMAS A.
There is so much natural beauty around us every day. We just have to take the time to stop and look around us. I like to capture these beautiful moments in time with my camera. A veteran photographer, named Neal Barnes, commented that with this photograph, "You've done a good job capturing not only a sunset, but displaying a mood. This is what everyone hopes to capture on film, but so few actually do at the level that you have. So, be proud of this one." I am!

WORLEY, BOBBY RAY
Eleven-month-old Dakota "Cody" Ray Worley loves his best buddy, Punky, later known as John Deere, even though he wasn't green. Cody developed a kinship with tractors and animals and so did Punky. Looks like they both may be farmers as well as best buddies for life.

WRIGHT, MEGAN
This is a photograph of what I call "The Grinning Crocodile." I took this photo in Florida when I went on vacation for two weeks. Actually, I thought the photo would not turn out too great, but it did! I am only eleven years old and I have two sisters named Kristen and Caitlin. I am in the sixth grade and love reading, basketball, and soccer. I also have two llamas named Willoughby and Safwa Wright. I enjoy and love taking photographs!

WRIGHT, NANCY LYON
Burlingame State Park in Rhode Island is a wonderful place to rest while enjoying God's creation. It was from a vantage point along a quaint dirt road in the park that we watched the sun find its way to the horizon. The awesome color spread across the sky, silhouetting the lone evergreen, which seemed to point majestically toward the heavens, reminding us of God's great glory. I dedicate this picture to my mom, Alice Lyon, who still enjoys a great sunset.

WYSONG, JENNA
In the simple intricacy of nature, I often feel God's presence most acutely. The beauty of the world He created and sustains reminds me of His love and mercy. This picture was taken along the creek in the woods near my house. In this wintry moment, time seemed overpowered by a sense of God's immortal nature and the everlasting love He has for every one of us. I love to take pictures of nature because for an instant in the right place at the right time, I can capture a glimpse of God's glory.

XIMEREZ, SABRINA
This beautiful breathtaking picture was captured while I was on the road with my family at the age of sixteen. It was taken while my hair was blowing in the wind at seventy miles per hour looking out into the Pacific coast. I was soaking in the moment forever that I wanted to soon share with everyone. At the same time, I was hoping my camera wouldn't fall on the road and shatter my picture. This was one of my first photos I ever took. This exact photo was the inspiration that spoke out to me and pushed me to pursue my passion.

YOUNG, JUDITH
We were in Florida on the Gulf to celebrate our fortieth wedding anniversary. We had a room overlooking the Gulf and when the sun began to set, I started taking pictures and this picture is my favorite. This picture won a blue ribbon at our local 4-H fair. It also hung at the Indiana State Fair and at the Honeywell Center in Wabash, Indiana. It has also been given as a gift. When I look at the picture, it reminds me of the beauty of God's creation.

YOUNG, MARGIE
This picture was taken only once. The car never displayed such glorious beauty again. Mother Nature designed this amazing design of frost. I had a truck beside the car and it had the design too. The car and truck never displayed a work of art again. Looking at this design, I knew it was a wondrous sight to behold. To me this was a very spiritual and sacred sight made especially for me.

ZEIEN, ALICIA
This is a photo of my cousin, Jessica. When I take pictures, I try to capture the emotion of the people. Also, I try to catch people when they don't realize a picture is being taken. That usually makes the picture more exciting and actually makes the photo worth a thousand words. I took this photo because I could sense the feelings she had in this picture. I feel that I captured her reflecting on the memories made in the pasture, which is how I thought of the title.

ZEINER, POLLY A.
While visiting the Iowa State University Butterfly Conservatory, trying to find the right butterfly was nearly impossible as they were flitting in the sunlight, as only a butterfly can. While resting for a minute, I watched this butterfly settle down as if he had enough airtime and wanted to be observed in his moment of glory. It was then that my moment of glory to observe the stillness he exhibited and allowed me to capture a "Butterfly At Rest." I only had one chance as this magnificent creature once again flitted off into the sunlight.

ZRECZYCKI, EVA LEONE
Currently I work as a registered nurse in a major Melbourne based hospital and as a hobby I have always been interested in digital photography, especially macrophotography. This photo is an example of close-up photography that shows us another world that we often take for granted and walk past without noticing. It was taken in my garden last summer and I hope it gives everyone who looks at it as much pleasure as it has given me.

INDEX OF PHOTOGRAPHERS

X

Y